Growing Vegetables and Herbs

Roger Grounds

WARD LOCK LIMITED · LONDON

Laminated Paperboard ISBN 0 7063 5361 7
Paperback ISBN 0 7063 5363 3

First published in Great Britain in 1977
by Ward Lock Limited, 116 Baker Street,
London, W1M 2BB.
A member of the Pentos Group.

Text filmset in Times Roman (327)

Printed Offset Litho and bound by
Cox and Wyman Ltd,
London, Fakenham and Reading

Contents

1 Introduction

Never before has it made more sense to grow your own vegetables than now. You can save a tremendous amount, especially in winter when you'd be buying frozen from the supermarket—and you'll get pleasure from your success into the bargain. To give you an example, from the £1 or so you pay out to buy a packet of lettuce seeds and the few other necessary odds and ends to grow them, you can get enough lettuce, fresh and crisp, to save up to £24 a year. And with something like runner beans, which would be bought frozen more likely than not, you could save as much as £43. That's worked out on last year's prices—and though the initial outlay will increase next year, it won't increase nearly as much as the price of vegetables in the shops. The 1976 drought will see to that as will the very wet winter of 1976 and the cold wet spring of 1977.

Apart from the money-saving side of it, it really is true that home-grown produce tastes better. The growers have different criteria from ours: what they want is vegetables that keep well and look good. What we want is fresh, flavourful produce that is conveniently ready at the right time and gives us many hours of pleasant occupation in the garden. So what's held you back so far? Probably just the thought that it's a bit too much trouble and you don't really know if you've got room. By the time you've read the first part of the book you'll be convinced you can do it, because all that is needed for success is the basic knowledge and practical guidance supplied here—then read on into part two for details about the different vegetables you'll want to try.

PLANNING

Go out into your garden and look at it. See how big it is. See what's there already. Make up your mind whether there is a spare patch of land already where you could grow your vegetables. Whether you're going to use a bit that is already lawn or flowerbed, or whether you're so enthusiastic you feel like clearing the lot out and starting from scratch with nothing but vegetables. There's no reason why you can't even grow some vegetables in among the other plants—your neighbours may be a bit amused, but so what?

Once you have decided how serious you are about growing vegetables, it won't take you long to decide how much space you're going to give them, but first you need to know roughly how much room you'll need and how many plants you can

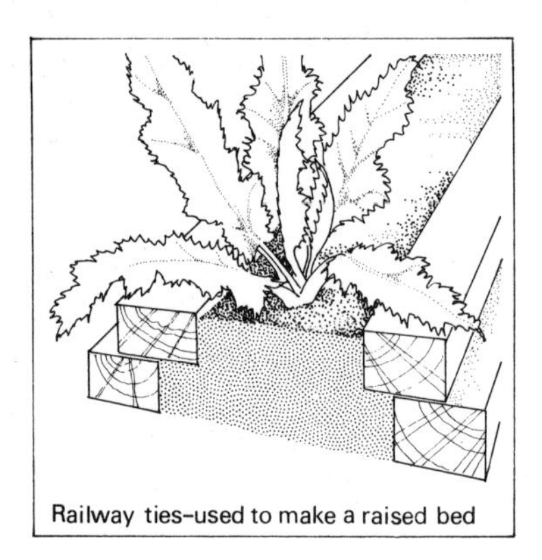
Railway ties–used to make a raised bed

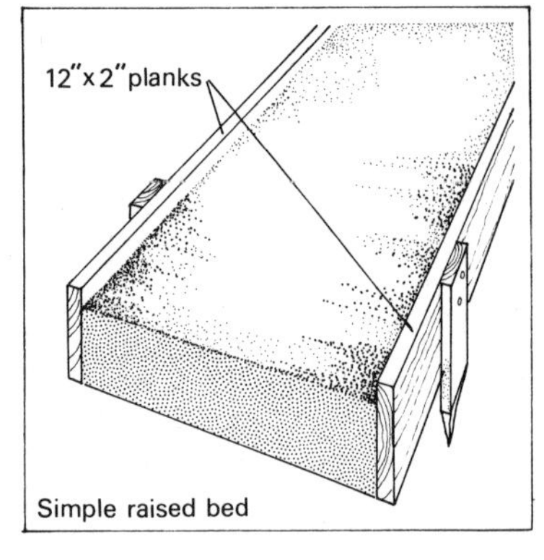

Simple raised bed

Stepped raised bed – gives you room to grow shallow and deep rooting crops at different levels

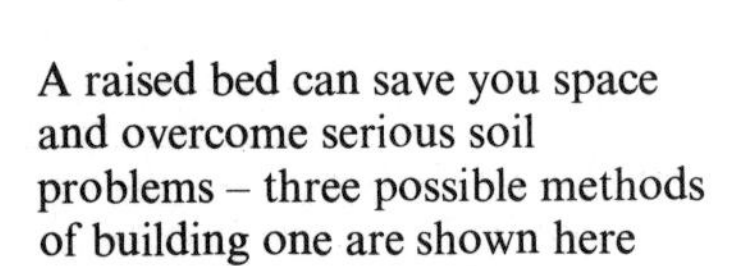
A raised bed can save you space and overcome serious soil problems – three possible methods of building one are shown here

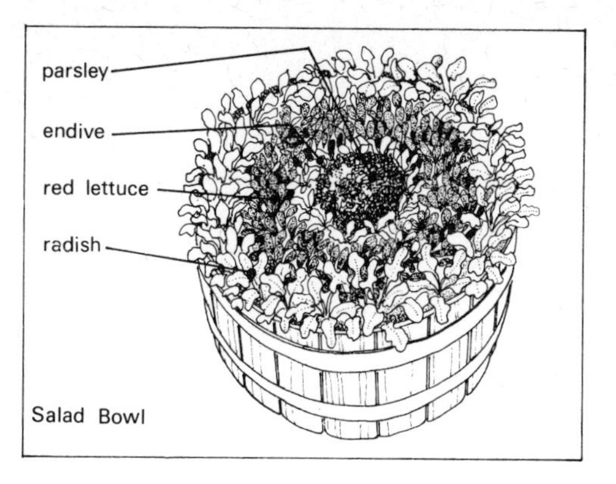

A decorative and space-saving idea for the tiny garden

fit into that space of the sort you'd like. So take a look at one or two of the vegetable sections in the later part of this book. At the bottom of each you'll find two figures—one telling you how much space is best left between each plant to avoid overcrowding and the other how much space you need between the rows of plants.

It is best if the row runs north/south, to catch the sun, so work out the most convenient way of arranging the rows with this in mind. Short rows leading off a central path at right angles are easy to get to, better than long rows running parallel.

Then you can plan an area of ground, if you have enough, for the compost heap. You will see at a glance how useful compost is if you read a bit of Section 2. A compost bin within reach of the vegetable patch and the house too will mean that you can make good use of all the weeds and trimmings from your vegetable growing and the left-overs such as peelings from the kitchen. A bonfire is a good idea too, as bonfire ash is rich in plant foods that encourage firm growth and good colour.

Rather than just trample the mud down along the paths between your vegetables, why not plan a proper path of bricks, concrete, cobbles or paving slabs? They'll need to be about 3 ft/1 m wide.

If you keep records of the vegetables you grow and where, you will find it easy to follow a system of crop rotation. This is a good idea because the plants will benefit from a change of ground for two reasons—you are reducing the chance of the soil being infested with pests and diseases common to a particular vegetable, and you are making sure that the soil has a chance to regain the particular plant foods that were taken out by the last crop. Furthermore, changing the vegetables round not only maximizes what you have spent on fertilizers and manures, but actually adds some nutrients for free.

For example, the Brassica family, cabbage, sprouts and so on, take a lot of nitrogen from the soil, while beans and peas *add* nitrogen, so the obvious thing to do is rotate the crops so that one group of vegetables can profitably follow the other. The chart suggests a simple plan for crop rotation, with your vegetables divided into three groups.

CROP ROTATION CHART

First year ABC
Second year CAB
Third year BCA

OTHER CROPS A	Beans, Celery, Corn, Cucumbers, Leeks Lettuces, Marrows and Squashes, Onions, Peas, Peppers, Pumpkins, Spinach, Tomatoes	*Add compost and/or manure*
ROOT CROPS B	Beets, Carrots, Potatoes, Radishes, Seakale beet	*Add fertilizer*
BRASSICAS C	Broccoli, Cabbages and Savoys, Cauliflowers, Kale, Kohlrabi, Sprouts	*Add fertilizer and lime*

After each vegetable section you'll get a reminder of which group that vegetable is in.

SOIL

Whatever kind of soil you've got you'll probably wish you had some other. Loam is about the best, but any of the soil types can be made productive with the right treatment.

Clay soils drain badly because the particles are too fine and let water through. In extreme cases, where surface water lies in great puddles, you'll have to lay land drains, but normally all you need do is add coarse sand and peat or compost in equal quantities by bulk. If you cover the area you intend to cultivate with a 2–3 in/5–7·5 cm layer, and dig this into the top 9 in/23 cm of soil, mixing soil, sand and compost together thoroughly, you'll have a highly workable soil your first year. So keep up a regular programme of improvement for three or four years and the most intractable clay will turn into a good loam. Once you've got it in the state you want it in, keep adding **humus**, preferably in the form of compost, every year, otherwise the soil will revert to its former clayey state.

Sandy soils need even less work than clay soils. Their main problem is that they drain too fast, which in turn means that all the goodness is washed out of them so that you have drought problems in summer. What they need is masses of humus in the recipe here—you just can't add too much. Dig anything from 3–6 in/7·5–15 cm of peat, leaf-mould, compost or manure into the soil each year for three years. Then keep adding lesser quantities every year thereafter. One of the problems of sandy soils is that they are usually lying over a sandy substructure, so that the humus you put in just keeps getting washed down to the layers below. That's why you have to keep adding humus.

Loam soils are good, workable soils to begin with. They generally do not need improving. Just work them carefully, adding a 2 in/5 cm layer of humus each year to replace what you take away from the ground in the way of crops, otherwise they will deteriorate.

Getting the PH right

Soil acidity or alkalinity—the concentration of hydrogen in the soil—is determined by the pH scale. Use a soil-testing kit and find out what sort of soil you have.

Vegetables grow best when the pH is *neutral* or slightly on the acid side, roughly pH6 or pH7. You may be lucky enough to have the right pH to start with, but still test it at least once every five years because cropping and fertilizing will gradually change the soil pH: peat will make the soil more acid, lime will make it more alkaline.

To correct an acid soil (pH6 or below), add lime. The problem is always to know at what rate to apply it, as this will vary considerably. For example, a quick-draining sandy soil will take less lime than a loam soil to raise the pH from 4·5 to 5·5, and to raise the pH of a clay by the same amount it will take even more lime. It is best to seek expert advice. Don't take the word of your garden centre—they will naturally want to sell you as much as they can.

There are several types of lime available. The most commonly used is hydrated lime. The best is ground Dolomite limestone, which lasts longer in the ground and also contains some magnesium, which many soils lack.

To make an alkaline soil more acid keep digging in moss peat. It is impossible to give accurate rates of application, again since the pH of the peat varies. Test the soil every year until you get the pH right.

But don't be put off by all this science. Vegetables are very tolerant of widely varying soils. Try to get your soil as neutral as you can, but don't worry about the odd decimal point on the pH scale. Alternatively, try everything, and then concentrate on what you find grows well in your particular soil.

Changing Your Soil pH in Relation to Your Soil Type

pH	SOIL ACIDITY	LIGHT SANDY SOILS	SANDY LOAM OR SILT SOILS	MEDIUM LOAM SOILS	CLAY LOAM SOILS	HEAVY CLAY SOILS
6·0	Moderate	2 lbs	3 lbs	4 lbs	5 lbs	5½–6 lbs
5·5	Strong	3 lbs	4 lbs	5¾ lbs	7 lbs	7¾ lbs
5·0	Very strong	3¾ lbs	5¾ lbs	7¼ lbs	8 lbs	9¼ lbs
4·5	Extreme	4 lbs	6½ lbs	8 lbs	8¾ lbs	10 lbs

Amount of hydrated lime required to raise pH 6·5, the optimum level. Rate per 100 sq ft.

FEEDING

The most important plant foods are hydrogen, oxygen and carbon. Plants get these from the air and water available to their roots in the soil. That is why a good soil structure is so important—you can't actually supply the plants themselves with hydrogen, oxygen and carbon, but you can make sure the soil has the best structure you can give it.

Then there are a number of minerals which plants get from the soil and absorb through their roots in the form of weak salt solutions. Three of them are more important than the rest: nitrogen, phosphorus and potassium. Nitrogen is essential to all plant growth, and important for increasing the bulk of the green part of the plant. Potassium is used for flowering and fruit-setting. Phosphorus helps plants grow the right colour. Calcium is almost as important, and occurs naturally in most soils—plants use it to build their cell walls. Provided your soil pH is right you should have no problem with calcium. In acid soil the calcium is usually present but lime is needed to release it.

Apart from these foods, there are micro- or trace elements, and all sorts of rare metals and minerals, but you needn't worry about these. There is usually enough in the soil.

There are two ways you can feed your plants to make sure they are getting the right things—with artificial fertilizers and with organic manure. Each has its advantage and disadvantage. Artificial fertilizers can be applied in exact quantities and you know just what is in them—but you are not building up humus. Organic manures do build up a supply of humus—but you do not know what proportions of the foods they contain. So ideally, use a combination of both.

Another important difference is that many artificial fertilizers release their food as soon as they combine with the moisture in the soil, but organic manures generally release their foods slowly and this is better because the plants are then fed over a longer period. For example, you can give plants nitrogen in the form of sodium nitrate, a chemical providing instant food, or you can give it to them in the form of dried slaughterhouse products, which is organic, and will release nitrogen slowly as it decays.

The prime plant foods are all contained in 'complete' fertilizers with a statement on the packet of the proportions of each—nitrogen is symbolized by the letter N, phosphorus by P and potassium by K: 10–10–10 on a packet would mean 10 per cent of each, in that order.

More often now, manufacturers are adding trace elements too, mainly iron, magnesium and manganese, but this is only in case they *happen* to be needed and it is rather a waste of money if they are not.

Always read the packets carefully. Don't give more than is necessary—the surplus won't store in the soil, it will just get washed away by the rain.

As for organic manures, they are not so easy to get hold of but can still be worth the search. To give you an idea of the approximate N, P, K content of some of them, blood and bone has 6·5 per cent N, and 7 per cent P, cow manure has 0·6 per cent N, 0·4 per cent P and 0·3 per cent K and garden compost has 1·5 per cent N, 2·0 per cent P and 0·7 per cent K.

This last is what people are turning to more and more with the others only available in the country areas. So you will need a bit of guidance on how to make your own compost in the garden.

The heap or bin is best situated in between the house and the vegetable plot as you will be using refuse from both these quarters. The sorts of thing to use are weeds, lawn clippings, leaves and burnt twigs, bonfire ash, vegetable leftovers and peelings, even vacuum dust and shredded paper. Anything that is basically organic.

You can add an activator to speed up the process if you like. There are many brands available. The purpose is to help feed the bacteria in the heap which break down the green material into that rich brown compost you want. Keep the heap always damp but never wet. In high rainfall areas keep it covered, and in winter too. Just use black plastic sheeting weighted down with bricks or rocks. Aim for the consistency of a squeezed out sponge.

During a two week period, the compost should reach a temperature high enough to kill off all the weed seeds and pests and diseases (about 150°F/65°C) but if it gets too hot the contents will become a sludgy mess. You'll know when it is ready from the following signs—the temperature will drop, it will start smelling fresh and earthy, it will be dark brown in colour and crumble between your fingers.

WATERING

All plants need water—but especially vegetables. Plants need this water to absorb their foods in the form of a weak solution, and in fact a good proportion of every plant is nothing but water—96 per cent of a cauliflower and 89 per cent of a stick of broccoli, for instance.

Vegetables absorb the water through their roots in the soil. Once the soil dries out, the reverse happens, and the soil starts to absorb water from the plants—then we have drought. At the other extreme, too *much* water in the soil and the vegetables will drown—they need air just as much as water. If all the air passages in the soil are full of water, the roots die off and rot sets in.

So what most vegetables need is an even supply of water, and water plus air in the same proportions. Just how much water you give your plants and how often depends on two things. Firstly, on what sort of soil you have. You need to water more often on a sandy, quick-draining soil than on a heavy, moisture-retaining clay soil. Secondly, it depends on whether the vegetable in question is deep- or shallow-rooting. For example, lettuce is a shallow-rooting vegetable, maximum depth of root 18 in/45 cm. On good loam you would water it every 5–7 days (about a large cupful), on sandy soil every 2–3 days and on clay every 8–9. Other shallow-rooting vegetables include broccoli, cabbage, celery, potatoes, spinach and sprouts, while among the deeper-rooting kind are leeks, onions and tomatoes.

The traditional method of watering plants is with a watering can. In fact this is not ideal, because a concentrated dose of water in one place tends to compact the soil and wash it away from the roots. Far better are the various types of sprayer and sprinkler you can buy. The mist-like spray is the nearest imitation of rain you can get and penetrates the soil very effectively.

Another effective method in hot dry weather is a seep hose. It is made of flat plastic stitched together in such a way that the water seeps through the stitching.

Now that drought conditions are unfortunately a part of our experience, it is worth your while considering what you would do when the ordinary water supply becomes so valuable that there are limitations on its use and you are forbidden to water your vegetables. One thing you can do is store used household water and re-use it in a purified form. For this process you'll need a 37-gallon/170 litre water butt to collect it in and a plastic cistern (15 gallon/70 litre). The water must trickle from one to the other, the filter cistern containing the following materials—6 in/15 cm charcoal, 6 in/15 cm very sharp sand, 3 in/8 cm fine gravel and a top layer of large pebbles. Allow the water to trickle out of this cistern at the same rate as it does from the butt, and gather the filtered water

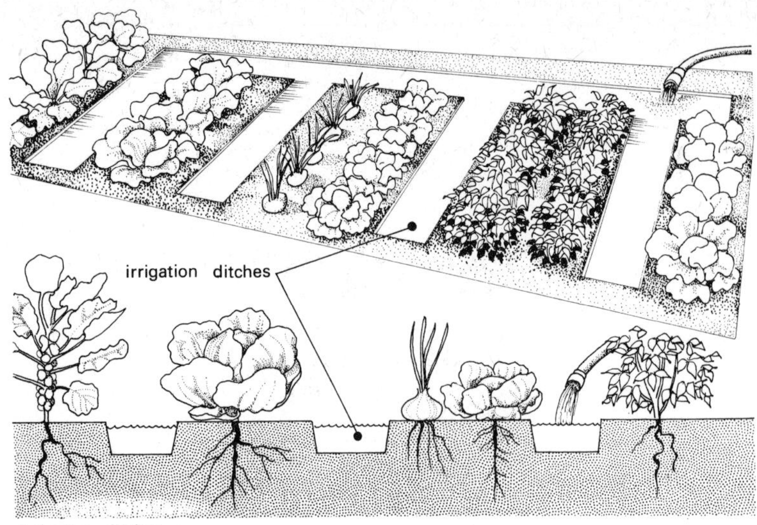

Irrigation ditches

If you live in a dry area, irrigation ditches will be useful – the subsidiary channels can be blocked with a plank if there are no plants to be watered growing alongside

in a series of linked butts—as many as you have space and money for if the drought looks like being long.

Again use a seep hose running from the butt. Place it as close to the roots as possible and cover with a mulch of peat or compost. You'll then get a constant steady supply of water for your vegetables without having to worry about them.

RAISING SEED OUTDOORS AND IN

A seed needs only two things to start it into life—an even flow of moisture, and warmth. Broadly speaking, you sow 'hardy' seed outdoors, so if you want to grow 'tender' vegetables such as cucumbers or peppers use a frame or the house; or give an early start to others, start them indoors and put them outside later.

Outdoors

Rough dig the soil in autumn, working in plenty of compost or organic manure. Once the ground is frost free, fork the top

Runner beans are one of the most prized of all summer vegetables. Well-grown beans are long and straight, but it takes a rich, deep soil to produce beans as good as these. *Courtesy W. J. Unwin Ltd.*

Young Brussels sprouts developing

A well-grown head of cabbage ready for harvesting

few inches over lightly in the spring. Then level and rake, breaking down any clods. Use the rake too, to remove stones, twigs and other debris. When ready the soil should have the top 2 in/5 cm loose and crumbly in texture, but not powdery.

Open a shallow slit in the soil, and scatter the seed in, just covering it with soil and gently tapping firm with the back of a rake or spade. With seeds that take a long time to germinate, it is important to keep the sprinkler moving over the rows, or the seeds may dry out and never appear. Label every row clearly, telling you what it is and the date you planted it.

Once the seedlings come through, thin them out to the recommended spacing. A common mistake with many vegetables is packing them so closely together that they rob each other of plant foods and the whole crop suffers.

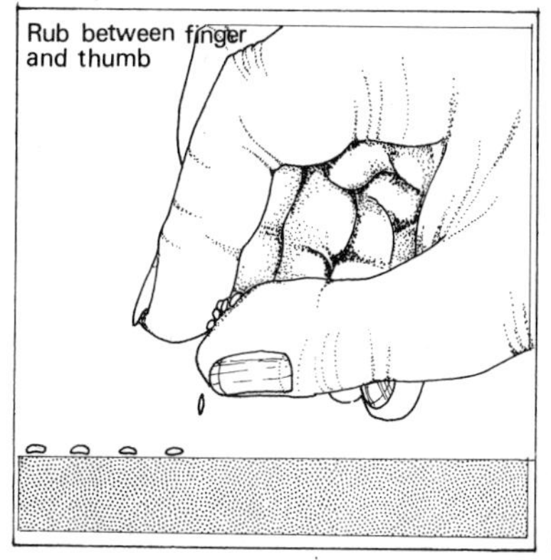

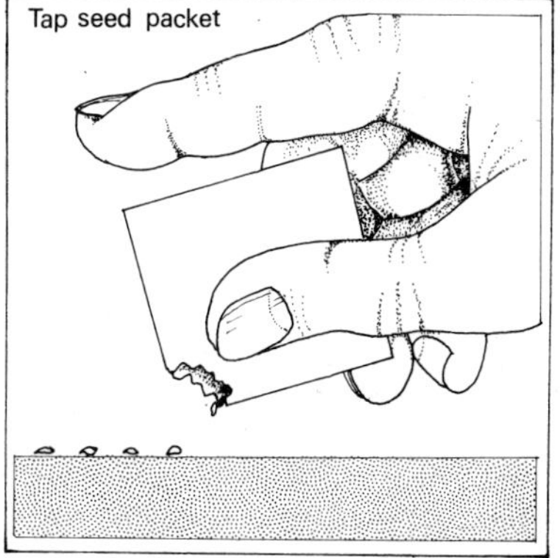

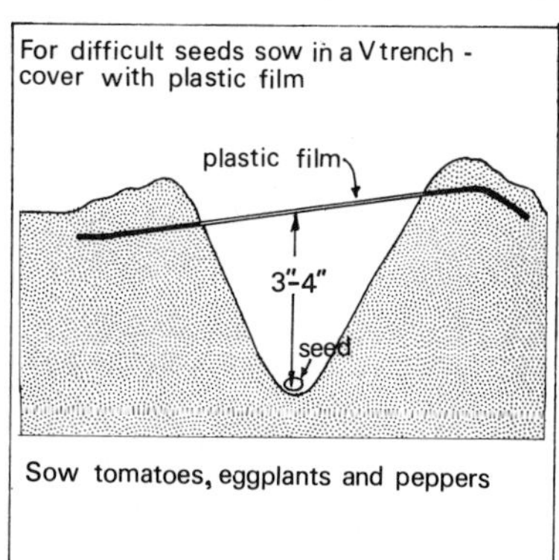

Three different methods of sowing seeds

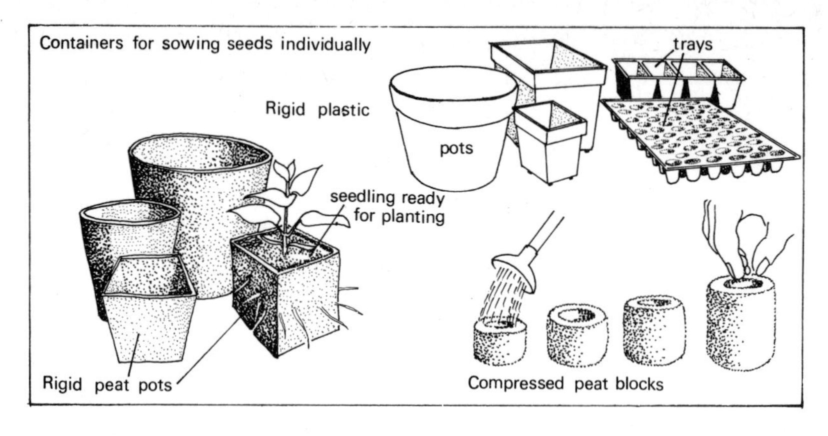

Any of the containers shown here are readily available from garden centres

Indoors

One of the best ideas in this case is to use compressed peat pots. They mean that you can transplant your seedling without disturbing its roots, as the whole pot is planted out just as it is. Fill the pots with a soilless growing mix and sow the seed in that. Once the roots start showing through the sides of the peat, it is time to plant out.

There are many small propagators designed for use in the

Thin wire and clear polythene are all that are necessary to make this simple propagator

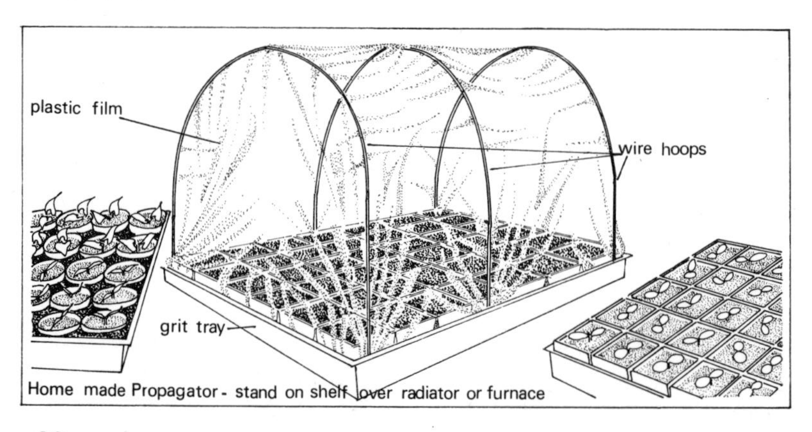

home. The simplest consists of a plastic tray with a clear plastic dome standing on a hotplate. Most designs raise the temperature up to 20 °F/6 °C above the room temperature. But if you haven't got a propagator like this to germinate seeds indoors, use a grit tray. Plant the seeds in their peat pots and put hoops of wire over the top. Then wrap the whole thing in clear plastic film. Stand it on the boiler or on a shelf over a radiator. Take the temperature inside the case with a thermometer to be sure it isn't getting too high.

Hardening off

Seeds raised in propagators or under glass need to be 'hardened off' before they can stand up to outside conditions. This is done by gradually getting them used to colder air.

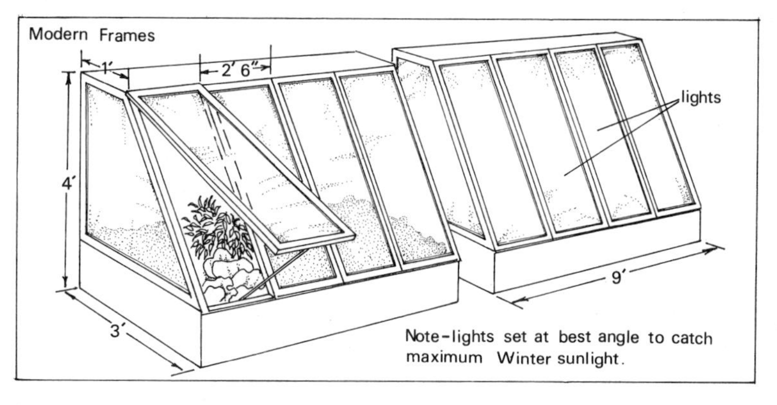

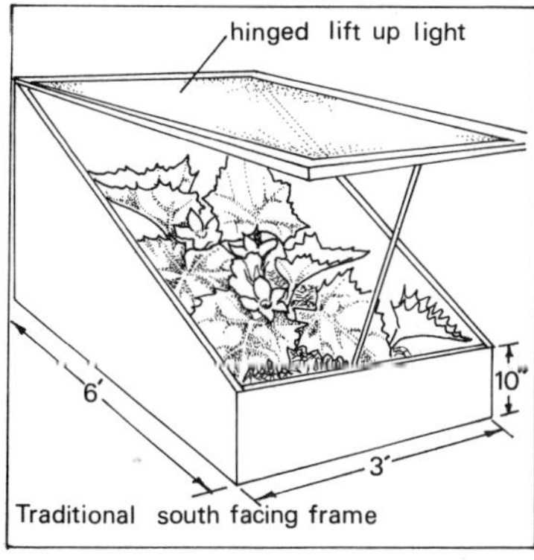

A cold frame is useful for hardening off plants raised indoors, and for growing some comparatively tender vegetables

Propagators usually have vents you can open a little at a time. But with the home-made type you'll get the same result by making a few holes in the plastic, then a few more the next week, and so on. Finally remove the roof or plastic film altogether for a while, then move them to a sheltered position outdoors. Still keep the seedlings protected though—close to a house wall. Put a pane of glass at a slant over the seedlings by night and if severe frost threatens, move them to a frame or even back inside (in the coolest part of the house though) till danger is past.

Transplanting

Seedlings started indoors should be hardened for about two weeks out of doors before being set in the soil. If you've grown them in a light, sandy growing mix, such as a soilless growing mix, don't put them straight into heavy clay and expect them to keep growing well. Dig plenty of light sandy soil into the planting position. Open a hole with a trowel large enough to put the peat pot or root ball in without having to squeeze or distort it. Return the surface soil and make it firm. Water lightly.

Protecting seedlings

Even at this stage, most seedlings are still vulnerable to extreme weather. So cover the transplants with a cloche. These will keep cold winds off, protect the plants from frost, and also act as a guard against birds, cats and dogs.

There are two types of cloche generally available, glass and plastic. The glass ones are probably best for the plants, the plastic ones for you. The panes in the glass cloches mean that you can remove as many as you like to increase ventilation when temperatures rise suddenly. It gives the plants less of a shock than if you suddenly take the whole lot off at once. The main disadvantage though is that you may break panes, you have to store them and generally they require a bit more effort. The plastic cloches or tunnels are easier to handle and can be bought or made.

If you are going to save some money and make your own, this is how you do it. Just push half-hoops of 11 gauge wire into the soil over the seedlings, and lay plastic sheeting over the

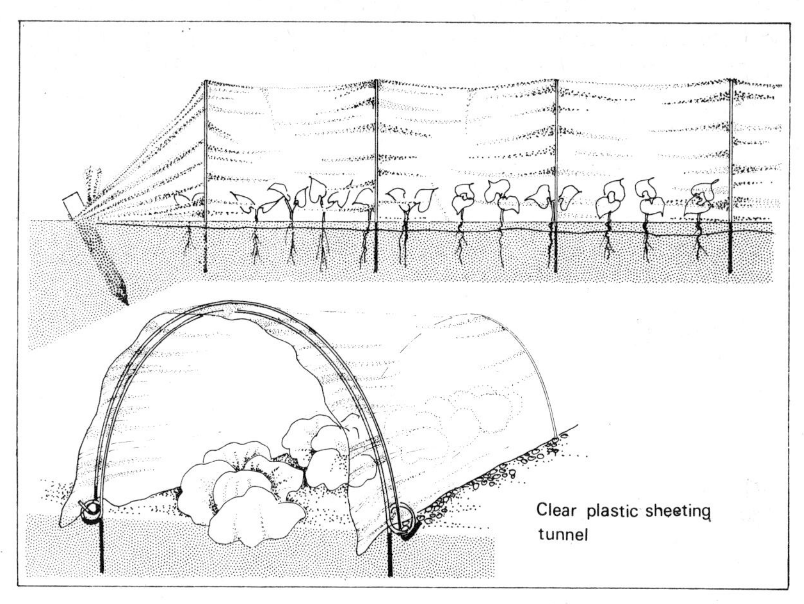

Cloches will protect seedlings and bring forward harvest dates

hoops, pulling it taut. Cut the sheeting 1 ft/30 cm wider than you need it. Lay 6 in/15 cm flat on the ground and cover with earth or bricks to weight it down, stretch the plastic sheeting taut over the hoops, then use the other spare 6 in/15 cm the same way on the other side, weighting it down to secure it. If you want to seal the ends, just gather the plastic sheeting together, tie a knot in it, string it to a tent peg and hammer the tent peg into the ground. Alternatively, loop the sheeting round the end half-hoops and staple it to itself, and then seal the ends with a sheet of rigid plastic or glass. You can then ventilate when you need to, or keep the tunnel ventilated and merely seal it when severe frosts threaten.

Feeding seedlings

First of all, keep an eye on soil moisture level. If the soil seems to be drying out, water is needed. But check that it isn't only the top ½ in/1·3 cm that is dry, by pushing a trowel into the soil. If it comes out moist, the soil is probably O.K.

Transplants should be fed two to three weeks after planting out. Use a mixture of balanced artificial fertilizer (to give instant food) and organic manure (to give a mulch and slower feeding). The mulch effect helps prevent soil from drying out by preventing upward evaporation. Apply the mixture either in 6 in/15 cm strips down each side of the rows, no closer than 3 in/7·5 cm to the seedlings, or, for large-growing plants, put it in a ring, again 3 in/7·5 cm away and 1 ft/30 cm wide.

DEALING WITH THE ENEMY

Weeds

Weeds are always a problem in the vegetable garden. If you're growing vegetables in open ground, every time you turn the soil you inevitably bring up more weed seeds. They were buried too deep to germinate: you bring them to the surface and they germinate. Then they rob your vegetables of valuable water and plant foods. If you let them continue to grow they'll completely smother your seedlings. So get rid of them!

There are three ways you can try. You can use pre-emergence weedkillers, which are often very effective. But one problem is that chemicals can be restricted by law and this keeps changing—so consult your local horticultural advisor. Keep them in locked cupboards, away from children or pets.

The traditional way of course is the hoe. You use a Dutch hoe with a push–pull action, cutting the weeds off under the surface of the soil, or you use a hook or draw hoe, with a chopping motion. Hoe at least once a week.

Then there are mulches, which are highly recommended because at the same time they conserve soil moisture by slowing down the rate of evaporation. Suitable materials for mulching are peat, well rotted compost, spent hops, sawdust, pine needles, ground pine bark or black plastic sheeting.

Pests—and Diseases

The longer a plant has been in cultivation, all over the world, the more pests and diseases are likely to attack it. And since vegetables are the longest cultivated of all plants, they have many enemies. Some are animals, like rabbits and mice. Many are insects, like aphids, caterpillars and cabbage root flies. Some are diseases, like moulds and fungi and bacteria.

But not all animals and insects are threats. Many work on our side. So use a book to identify them and then check up whether they are friend or foe. The best way to deal with enemy insects and diseases is to *prevent* them from ever appearing. There are several ways of keeping them at bay:

1) Weed out the sickly plants.
2) Keep weeds down—they provide a perfect breeding place.
3) Remove rotting vegetation, twigs and so on *at once*. Put it in the compost bin.
4) Grow disease-resistant varieties or sow disease-treated seed.
5) Rotate crops (*see* page 10, Planning) to keep the soil healthy.
6) Encourage those insects and animals that are not enemies.
7) Grow companion crops, like tomatoes with asparagus—they keep down aphids—or rosemary, sage, thyme, nasturtium, catmint or hyssop near a cabbage plot as they keep down cabbage white butterflies.

If you are sure there are enemy bugs on your vegetables, the options open are:

1) Squash them between fingers and thumb.
2) Squirt them with a hose or spray gun, to drown them.
3) Spray them with something like vegetable oil or milk, to suffocate them.
4) Use chemicals such as derris, pyrethrum or malathion (*not* DDT) as a last resort, but with extreme care—unless you want to kill your pets as well as pests! Particularly bear in mind that fish can easily be poisoned through the water.

THE MOST COMMON CROP SPOILERS AND WHAT TO TREAT THEM WITH

Name	Treatment
Aphid—eats almost anything.	Pyrethrum or malathion.
Slug—most vegetables, especially those close to the ground.	Methiocarb, metaldehyde granules.

Damping off—seedlings of most plants. Also called pythium.	Pre-treat seeds with copper fungicide or apply thiram once they emerge.
Botrytis—almost all crops.	Captan, thiram or Benlate.
Caterpillar—all crops.	Derris, Gamma BHC.
Cabbage root fly—cabbage, cauliflower, kale, kohlrabi.	Diazinon, Gamma BHC.
Club root—cabbage, cauliflower, kale, kohlrabi.	Apply calomel dust to soil. Rotate crops regularly.

STORING AND FREEZING

Most of the vegetables you are likely to want to grow can be stored successfully, given the right conditions. Exceptions are ripe tomatoes and greens. Marrows, pumpkins, onions, peas and beans store best under *dry*, cool conditions. But the rest like dark, cool (temperature around 32°F/O°C), well-ventilated places with a high humidity: such as a cellar, attic, unheated garage or shed.

The best thing to keep them in is a chest-of-drawers structure that you can make for yourself without too much trouble, from 2 × 1 in/5 × 2·5 cm slats. Cover the outside with hardboard. Nail fine-gauge wire over the outside as a protection against mice and birds. Then make the drawers quite deep, at least 6 in/15 cm, giving them fine-gauge wire bottoms for good ventilation.

Keep the humidity of the room high by placing a large bowl of water in there.

Freezing

Refer to the last chapters of this book for the length of time needed to blanch each vegetable, because this is a process involved in the freezing. (After washing and cutting up your vegetables, you will have to plunge them for the set number of minutes into a pan of boiling water and then into cold water for the same number of minutes.) This blanching stops the enzyme action that is going on in the vegetables, and so stops it from ruining the taste and texture.

When the chunks or slices have been drained, put them into freezer containers, usually plastic bags, and get rid of as much air as you possibly can. There are two good tricks to help with this: either suck the air out with a straw or dunk the bag in water, so that the water pressure pushes out the air and you get a vacuum in the bag. Then seal the neck of the bag, label it and place it in the deep freeze.

The label should state the name of the vegetable and the date on which it was placed in the freezer. If you like keeping records, you may want to keep a chart on the side of the freezer, telling you what vegetables you froze when, and on what date they were removed. That way you can see at a glance what you have in the freezer at any one moment. The records also help you to know whether you could have managed on less or whether you needed more, and then next year you can change your plans a bit. Ideally, try to maintain a complete turnover of vegetables in your freezer every year. After that length of time, taste and texture might begin to deteriorate, but for up to a year home frozen vegetables will be a joy to eat.

2 The Vegetables

BEANS, DWARF FRENCH

Dwarf French beans give you more edible produce per unit area used than any other vegetable. They're easy to grow provided that you get the soil right. They like sun, sun and more sun and will yield well even in drought conditions.

Soil and sowing

Choose a sunny situation in the vegetable garden, and unless your soil is already light and sandy work in plenty of coarse sand and clinkers and some peat or compost to lighten the soil. At the same time work in 1½ oz of sulphate of potash per yard. Sow seed outdoors in June or under cloches in May. Take out a shallow drill 1 in/2½ cm deep, sow the seeds 4 in/10 cm apart, replace the soil and tread to firm. When the seedlings are 2 in/5 cm tall, thin to four plants per square foot.

Growing

Keep the hoe moving between the rows all through the growing season. After the first crop apply a general purpose fertilizer in bands at each side of the crop. Don't let the fertilizer touch the crop itself or it will burn it. Hoe the bands into the soil then water well in. This way you'll get a second crop—not so heavy as the first, but still worth having.

Harvesting

Harvest the beans while they are still young and succulent. A bean in perfect picking condition should snap when you break it. If it doesn't, it's too old to bother with. Harvest carefully, cutting the beans from the plant. Don't try to pull them off: chances are you'll pull the whole plant out of the ground.

Common mistakes

Sowing too early: seeds will not germinate in cold soil. Planting too deep. Failure to feed the crop: beans make rapid growth and need plenty of readily available nutrients if they are to grow and crop well. Failure to water: beans that are allowed to dry out abort.

ROTATION GROUP C

Space between plants 4 in/10 cm

Space between rows 12 in/30 cm

BEANS, RUNNER

This bean is one of the staple crops of the British home garden. Popularly known as the scarlet runner bean, there are in fact several varieties with white flowers. In full leaf and full pod the vines are heavy, so make sure the supports you put in are stout, strong and secure in the ground.

Soil

Unlike other beans, runner beans do best in a freshly manured soil. Prepare the soil by taking out a trench for each row. Add some compost or well-rotted manure plus hydrated lime. Return the soil and add some general purpose fertilizer. Then leave it for two weeks before inserting the poles. A series of T-poles set down the centre of the row, tied across the top by a single 2 × 3 in/5 × 7·5 cm piece of hardwood and supported by

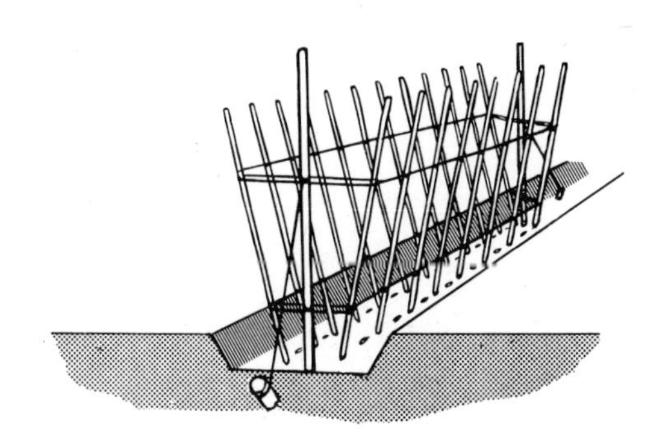

Runner bean supports need to be fixed securely

angle bars at each end will usually hold the crop. Poles should be 12 ft/4 m tall with 2 ft/0·5 m buried in the ground. Strings or wires should run from the outer edge of the Ts to the base of the poles.

Sowing

Sow seed in open ground in June, one at the foot of each string. Plant 2–3 in/5–7·5 cm deep. Or indoors in peat pots in late April/early May. Thin out seedlings—ideal spacing is five plants per square yard/metre.

Growing

Give the plants a mulch of compost or peat as soon as they are 3–4 in/7·5–10 cm tall. Keep well watered but never wet. The beans climb by twining, so tie back any dangling shoots on to the strings with raffia. When the first beans form, give a mulch of strawy manure or an artificial fertilizer. Spray the beans overhead at dusk or dawn to keep them tender.

Harvesting

Harvest when three-quarters catalogue length. Later and they'll get stringy.

Common mistakes

Allowing the soil to dry out. Overplanting—five plants per person is quite enough unless you intend to freeze some.

ROTATION GROUP C

Space between plants 4–6 in/10–15 cm

Space between rows 36–48 in/1–1·2 m

BEETS

Soil

In the wild, beets will grow right down the chalk cliffs and into the sand, so take a tip from that and give them a really sandy soil, all the sun they can get and literally—a pinch of salt. Use compost, moss peat, something like that to give them humus. But no manure or fertilizer.

Sowing

Sow outdoors where the plants are to grow in April to June.

Seed needs to be $\frac{1}{2}$–$\frac{3}{4}$ in/13–18 mm deep. It can also be sown under cloches or plastic tunnels a few weeks earlier. Beets are sometimes sold as seedballs with three to five seedlings on each. Thin these to one plant per seedball and leave 3–4 in/7·5–10 cm between plants.

Growing
When the beet tops are about 4 in/10 cm high, apply a mulch to keep the weeds down and feed with fertilizer. Keep the crop well-watered—it needs a steady supply of moisture through the whole growing season. And it's a crop that needs to grow fast to taste good, so don't slacken up on that watering schedule.

Harvesting
As soon as they are the size of golf balls, simply dig the beets out of the ground, trim off the tops (excellent for the compost bin) and wash the earth off. Never scrape off the earth as you might damage the skin and spoil the flavour of the beets.

Common mistakes
Planting in rich soils. Irregular watering. Lack of moisture at the roots. Not keeping competition down—even other beets you didn't have the heart to thin out are a threat because they are robbing the crop of valuable water at the root.

ROTATION GROUP B
Space between rows 18–24 in/46–60 cm
Space between plants 1–2 in/2·5–5 cm

BROCCOLI
Broccoli is one of the members of the cabbage family grown for its edible flowers rather than for its leaves, though it still comes under the rather vague term 'greens'. It is more closely related to the cauliflower than the cabbage, the main difference being that in the cauliflower the flower is produced in a compact head, while in broccoli it is in a series of little loosely-formed sideshoots. It is a perennial plant and can be left in the ground for several seasons, but for best results start the crop afresh every year, putting old plants on the compost heap.

Soil
Its soil needs are the same as those of cabbage—a well-worked soil with plenty of manure or compost dug in and a fertilizer worked thoroughly into the soil.

Sowing
Sow late April or May, ½ in/1·3 cm deep. Use a seedbed or sow where the plants are to grow—don't waste valuable frame, greenhouse or windowsill space on broccoli seed. It is hardy.

Growing
Even if you sow seed where the plants are to grow, it pays to lift and replant them because they are so tall-growing that they need to be set firmly in the soil. So put them in about 1 in/ 2·5 cm deeper in the soil than in the flats or seedbed and make the soil round them really firm. Do this about June or July. Keep weeds down with a mulch of peat or compost in a ring round the plants or in lines down the rows. Feed with ammonium nitrate/nitro-chalk worked well into the mulch about four weeks after planting out.

Harvesting
The flower heads are best harvested when they are small and not too well developed. They are far more tender like this. Remove the head at the top first, then pick the side-heads as and when you want them. Other side-heads will follow. You should be able to keep on harvesting from midsummer right through until hard frosts set in. In fact light frosts even improve the taste.

Common mistakes
Planting too shallowly: they fall over in the breeze then. If your soil is very friable don't be ashamed to stake your broccolis.

ROTATION GROUP C
Space between plants 14–18 in/35–46 cm
Space between rows 24–30 in/60–75 cm

CABBAGES AND SAVOYS
Cabbages are one of the easiest and hardiest of vegetables you

Savoys are at their best early in the year, and are very hardy

can grow. By nature they are biennials, forming their good, firm round heads the first year, then shooting up into flower the second year. If you choose your varieties carefully you can have cabbages ready to eat all year round.

Soil

Cabbages and savoys are greedy feeders, particularly demanding on nitrogen, so prepare the soil well to a depth of about 1 ft/30 cm, digging in plenty of manure or compost together with some artificial fertilizer, worked well in so as not to burn the roots.

Sowing

Cabbage seed can be sown at almost any time of year to produce a harvest at almost any season. For best results sow in several batches. Sow summer cabbages indoors ($\frac{1}{2}$ in/1 cm deep) in January. After, sow from March till May to harvest in July–November. Sow spring cabbage late July/

early August, transplant them to rows in September/October to harvest February–March.

If you buy transplants, small ones are the best value. Those with thicker stems are liable to bolt (run to seed) if temperatures drop.

Growing

Keep the plants weed-free by hoeing or using a mulch. Keep an eye on soil moisture content: cabbages grown under drought conditions are no good. Feed about four weeks after planting out or thinning with ammonium nitrate/nitro-chalk. It is now essential to take precautions against cabbage root flies. Routine control is with calomel paste. Or put a plastic collar around the stem—with better results than with any chemical.

Harvesting

Simply pluck the plants from the ground, cut off the roots and use these in the compost bin.

Common mistakes

Planting too many—only plant what you can use in a two to three week period.

ROTATION GROUP C

Space between plants 12–20 in/30–50 cm

Space between rows 24–30 in/60–75 cm

CARROTS

Carrots are native to most of Europe, including the British Isles. They're probably the easiest of all vegetables to grow. They're not too fussy about soil, though they prefer light, sandy soils, not too bothered about fertilizers either way, nor by climate.

Soil

Like all root crops, carrots do best in a patch of land that has been manured for a previous crop. Unless you want oddities avoid freshly manured soils.

Sowing

Unless you buy ready-treated seed, dress the seeds in gamma

Red cabbages like these are often known as pickling cabbages

Dwarf curly kale – a reliable winter vegetable for colder districts

Cauliflower 'Unwins Snocap', an extra early very large-heading variety *Courtesy W. J. Unwin Ltd*

To grow good carrots you need a carefully prepared, stone-free bed. Stones distort the shape of the carrot. Too rich a soil (i.e. one freshly manured) will make them split

BHC (HCH) dust by shaking them around in an envelope of half a teaspoonful of the stuff. Sow the seeds where the plants are to grow. Instead of the usual rows, 12 in apart, try broadcasting the seed and cover the seed with not more than $\frac{1}{4}$ in/6 mm soil or sand. Water the seed in. You can sow it any time from March till June, and it's best done in sequences, at two-week intervals.

Growing

They do not need much care. Just keep the soil weed-free and make sure the soil is always moist but not wet, or they'll rot. If you do use a feed, give only artificial fertilizers.

Harvesting

In light friable soils just pull the carrots out of the ground by their tops. In heavier soils lift them with a lifting fork. Start harvesting when the tops are about 2 in/5 cm high, when the carrots will be small and tender. Keep on harvesting till they're starting to get woody, then pull up the rest of that sowing, and start the next. Make sure you have all the carrots out of the ground before your first frost as it will ruin their flavour.

Common mistakes

Overplanting and underthinning. Planting in newly manured soil.

ROTATION GROUP B
Space between plants 1–2 in/2·5–5–5 cm
Space between rows 18–24 in/46–60 cm

CAULIFLOWERS

The general cultivation is the same as for the cabbage, but it is altogether a rather more difficult plant to grow well. It will not stand as much cold and it does not head up properly in hot summer regions.

Soil

Prepare the soil by taking out a 10 in/25 cm trench a spade-width across. Work in plenty of manure or compost plus some commercial fertilizer and lime.

Sowing

By carefully choosing the right variety and sowing it at the right time, it is possible to have heads of cauliflower all the year round, in phases:

PHASE 1: Seeds of the earliest varieties such as 'Snowball' are sown in frames in September or indoors in mild heat in January. After hardening off in March they are planted out in April to cut in May or June. Or sow outdoors in April for August.

PHASE 2: Varieties like 'All the Year Round' are a little later maturing, ready by June or July although sown and planted at the same time as above.

PHASE 3: Varieties such as 'Majestic' or 'Veitch's Self-protecting' can be sown outdoors from March to May to give firm mature heads from September to December.

PHASE 4: Australian varieties like 'Canberra' and 'South Pacific' are also sown in April and May and are ready in late autumn or winter.

PHASE 5: Winter cauliflower, sometimes called broccoli, matures from November to June and is sown outdoors from March to May and planted out in July.

Growing

Take standard cabbage root fly precautions and keep weeds down with a good mulch of compost. Six weeks after planting, apply a feed of ammonium nitrate/nitro-chalk, worked well into the mulch, and water heavily.

As soon as the heads start to show, start blanching. That is, gather the leaves together over the cauliflower head and tie them. Leave them for seven to ten days and then harvest.

Harvesting

Pluck the plants, slice off the roots, untie the leaves and cut them back to half their length.

Common mistakes

Overplanting and planting too close together in the rows.

ROTATION GROUP C

Space between plants 18 in/46 cm

Space between rows 30–36 in/75–90 cm

CELERY

Soil

Celery seedlings like soil that has been well-fed beforehand with artificial fertilizer. Work it in well as they will scorch if you leave it on top of the soil. It also helps to dig in plenty of manure or compost.

Sowing

Seed is tiny, so sow it not more than $\frac{1}{8}$–$\frac{3}{4}$ in/3–18 mm deep, indoors in March or April. Cover the flats or pots with newspaper or burlap to prevent rapid drying out. Once the seedlings show above the soil, cover with plastic sheeting held away with hoops. If sowing in open ground, do the same. The seeds and seedlings need plenty of moisture. Plant out seedlings in May or June, by which time they should be 2–3 in/5–7·5 cm tall. (Handle them carefully as the roots will easily snap.)

Growing

Keep the plants growing well by ensuring high soil moisture content. Mulching with organic materials can help to reduce evaporation and feed the plants too.

Modern self-blanching varieties do not need further blanching, but if you grow blanching varieties, here's how: either earth them up like potatoes or plant them in trenches 12–15 in/30–38 cm deep and fill the trenches instead of hilling. When the sticks are about 12–15 in/30–35 cm tall, gather the leafing tops together and tie them tightly with raffia or elastic bands. Then either hill the earth up or fill the trench with soil. Allow two months for blanching.

Harvesting

Harvest as needed from one end of the row to the other. Gourmets usually say celery needs a touch of frost to perfect its flavour.

Common mistakes

Trying to grow the sticks too tall. Earthing up the hills too high or making the trenches too deep. Avoid covering the green leafy part when blanching. Never let the plants lack moisture at the roots: the celery will be stringy.

Earthing up celery to blanch the stems

ROTATION GROUP A
Space between plants 8 in/20 cm
Space between rows 24–30 in/60–75 cm

CORN

If you've never tasted corn except from a supermarket deep freeze, shatter your taste buds by growing corn the way the Americans do. The only problem is that corn is a hot summer, long-season crop and doesn't take kindly to dull grey muggy British summers. You'll only ripen the ears if you grow short-stature, fast-maturing varieties. Keep an eye on catalogues for promising varieties.

Soil

Corn likes a light sandy soil, so if you need to improve yours, trench the ground in the autumn to 12–18 in/30–46 cm and dig in plenty of coarse sand, clinkers and peat. At the same time dig in barrowloads of compost or manure. Leave the soil over winter. Then in spring add some fertilizer.

Sowing

Sow indoors in April or May in a heated greenhouse, or frame or on the windowsill of a warm room which gets full sun. Sow in peat pots in soilless growing mix, two seeds per pot. Once they've germinated pluck out the weaker of the two. Keep the plants growing well but gradually harden them off for planting out in June. Keep them covered with cloches for four weeks, gradually letting more and more air in and finally remove the cloches. Corn is better planted in blocks than rows, as it is wind-pollinated and this gives the ears a better chance of getting pollinated.

Growing

Corn is a fast grower and a greedy feeder, so make sure at all times that there is plenty of fertilizer available for it. If the leaves go yellow there is a nitrogen deficiency: run to your nearest garden centre for a nitrogen-only fertilizer. Another important thing is to harden your heart and thin ruthlessly. More crops are ruined by overcrowding than anything else. Surplus seedlings rob the others of food just as much as weeds do. Ideally plants ought to be 10–14 in/25–35 cm apart. Keep weeds down with a good mulch of strawy manure or compost —never hoe the soil. And give the corn water, water, water, all the season round. Then double the water supply from tasselling time to harvest.

Harvesting

The problem here is knowing just when to pick the ears. When the female threads turn dark brown, ease the green bracts back gently—press one grain with the thumbnail and if the cob is ripe a white milky sap will emerge. Then snap out the cobs, remove the remaining female threads and bracts.

Corn is at its sweetest the moment you cut it from the plant. Within ten seconds the sugars have started to turn to starches. So have some water on the boil before you cut the ear. Don't boil it for more than five or six minutes though, otherwise you boil away the flavour.

Don't remove the husk till you're ready to cook or the kernels will taste terrible.

Common mistakes

Planting out too early in the hope of giving it a long growing season—if you get it off to a good start under glass you've already solved that problem. Failure to take action against corn earworm—incidentally, varieties with tight husks suffer less damage.

ROTATION CROP A
Space between plants 10–14 in/25–35 cm
Space between rows 30–36 in/75–90 cm

CUCUMBERS

Soil

Cucumbers need soil that is almost entirely humus. Most people grow them in hills. Dig a hole in the autumn 3 ft/1 m deep and 3 ft/1 m across and dump 1 ft/30 cm of well rotted farmyard manure or compost into it. As you fill back the soil, mix in more manure to make a hill 50/50 original soil and manure. Space the hills 2–3 ft/60–92 cm apart. If you haven't room to do this you could train the vine up a fence, pole or wall; or grow mini varieties in tubs, pots or boxes.

Sowing

Cucumbers are fast-growing short-season crops but they need plenty of heat, and in Britain summers cannot be counted on. This means that cucumbers need to be sown indoors in a heated greenhouse, in April or May. This goes for both ridge and frame types. Plant out in June and cover with cloches or plastic tents.

Growing

Regular spraying is required to keep down red spider. Cucumbers need a lot of moisture at the roots—they send down their roots as much as 3 ft/1 m, so give the water slowly so that it can soak down. They are acutely allergic to fertilizers so don't apply any—that's why it's so important to get plenty of good plant foods into the soil at the start. Keep hills weed-free with a mulch of compost, shredded pine-bark or any other high-humus/low-nutrient mulch. Skip the suggestions of pollinating cucumbers—the ones you need to pollinate taste bitter anyway. Grow the modern gynoecius types which are all female.

Harvesting

Harvest cucumbers at half the length the catalogues say—at full length they've lost their flavour, and anyway the more you harvest the more they produce.

Common mistakes

Planting too early. Letting them grow to full length. Not enough watering.

ROTATION GROUP A

Space between plants 12 in/30 cm or 3 per hill
Space between rows 48–72 in/1·2–2 m or 5 ft/between hills

KALE

Kale is yet another vegetable in the cabbage group. It is extremely hardy and often grown as 'winter greens' as it will survive frost levels that would ruin many similar crops. It is rather too strong-tasting for some people but you may like to try it. Grow it as a spring or autumn crop as it can't stand summer heat—the autumn crop is usually the best.

Soil
Plant in well-dug soil that has been manured for a previous crop, never in a freshly manured plot. It does best where the nutrient levels in the soil are high but balanced.

Sowing
Sow seed in April or May, about eight to ten per ft/30 cm, then thin to 8–12 in/20–30 cm between plants. Transplant in June or July.

Growing
Simply make sure the soil never dries out. Keep the weeds down with a mulch of compost or any other low-nutrient content organic substance.

Harvesting
Pluck the leaves with a sharp downward pull, when needed. After harvesting, put the haulms and roots in the compost.

Common mistakes
Trying to grow a good crop in hot weather.

ROTATION GROUP C

Space between plants 8–12 in/20–30 cm
Space between rows 18–24 in/46–60 cm

KOHLRABI
This is an oddity in the vegetable kingdom—a cross between a cabbage and a turnip. Odd though it may be, it tastes delicious, and even looks stunning growing in your garden. It is both subtler and sweeter than either of its relations.

Soil
Grow it in a soil that has been manured for a previous crop, not freshly manured—kohlrabi is in fact a root crop even though you grow it for the stem and it sits on top of the soil.

Sowing
Sow outdoors ½ in/1·3 cm deep first of all in March and right on till August. If you want an early start, sow indoors a month or so earlier. Transplant around May, taking care not to

Kohlrabi. The swollen stems appear above the soil, and should be harvested in good time

set the seedlings too deep or the swelling will occur underground and the stem be inedible.

Growing

Keep weeds down by moving the hoe between the rows: weed between the plants by hand. Be careful if you apply a mulch to suppress weeds because you might get it humped over the swollen part of the stem. Keep the soil moisture level quite high, but not wet or the stems will rot.

Harvesting

Pull the plants out and trim off the roots and leaves. Harvest when the stems have swollen to about 4–4½ in/10–11 cm in length, 3–3½ in/7·5–9 cm in diameter. You'll find there is a woody core to the kohlrabi, which becomes more noticeable the longer you leave them in the ground after the correct time to harvest.

Common mistakes

Underthinning. Manuring the soil. Harvesting too late when they have become woody.

ROTATION GROUP C
Space between plants 4–6 in/10–15 cm
Space between rows 18–24 in/46–60 cm

LEEKS

The simplest way to describe a leek is as an onion that does not form a bulb. The part you eat is called the stick, and is the stem. The aim of cultivating leeks is to make the stick as long and thick and tender as possible.

Soil

Grow in a soil previously manured, usually in permanent beds not rotated. What they like best is a deep, rich, well-worked soil, a good rich loam. In spring take out a trench one spade wide and 10 in/25 cm deep, throwing up half the soil on each side of the trench. Add a 2–3 in/5–7·5 cm layer of compost to the bottom of the trench, cover that with a 2 in/5 cm layer of soil and set your transplants into that.

Sowing

Sow seed outdoors when the plants are to grow in March or April, or for an earlier harvest, indoors or under cloches two to three months earlier. Set transplants out in May or June when they are about 3 in/7·5 cm tall. Make a hole in the bottom of the trench with a dibber and drop the plants in the hole. Do not firm—that makes them form bulbs. Thin to 12 in/30 cm in summer and use the thinnings to lace a salad or flavour the boiled greens.

Growing

Keep the trench free of weeds, preferably by hand—hoeing could damage the sticks. Don't use a mulch. Leeks can use plenty of water provided the soil is free-draining. Early in August put some corrugated paper round the sticks and from then on start earthing up, using the soil thrown to one side of the trench. The paper will start the blanching process and also help draw the leek. Also, clip off half the length of each leaf—this will help thicken the sticks. Keep on watering and earthing up, taking care not to get earth into the crown.

Harvesting

The sticks should be ready to harvest through October and November. Lift the leeks carefully with a fork and wash the soil away. Leeks can stay in the ground till you need them as long as Christmas or often beyond.

Common mistakes
Overfeeding. Over-blanching.
ROTATION GROUP A
Space between plants 2–4 in/5–10 cm
Space between rows 12–18 in/30–46 cm

LETTUCE (Butterheads, Crispheads and Cos)

There are two groups of lettuce, leaf and head lettuce and each group has two types. Head lettuces or cabbage lettuces can be Crispheads or Butterheads, and the leaf lettuces can be Bunching or Cos. Generally leaf lettuces have a slightly sharper flavour.

Soil
Lettuce likes a well cultivated soil with plenty of humus and plant nutrients, but as it is shallow-rooting you only need prepare the top 5–6 in/12·5–15 cm of soil thoroughly. Dig in all the humus material you can get.

BUTTERHEADS

Sowing
Sow indoors in January or February, prick seedlings off into small peat pots and plant under cloches in March ready for the open in April and a May/June harvest. Outdoors seed can be sown from March to July about every fourteen days to give you a succession of crops through to November. Seed of the hardy varieties can be sown in September to early October, left over winter with cloche protection, ready for the next May.

Growing
Do not let them dry out—liquid fertilizer would be a good idea in summer.

CRISPHEADS

Sowing
Sow ever two or three weeks from March to July. If you're short of space choose a small variety like 'Tom Thumb' and

space 6 in/15 cm apart, so as to pack them into a small plot: this variety is very good and crisp.

Growing
Liquid feed again if you want really giant heads.

COS
Sowing
Sow summer varieties indoors in January or February to plant out in March. Sow outdoors from March to July. If space is limited 'Little Gem' needs only 6 in/15 cm spacing and produces a crisp succulent heart.

Growing
Support the large-leaved types with raffia, string or elastic bands.

Harvesting
To test the firmness of head lettuces, use the back of the fingers to press gently down on the heart. Never 'pinch' a heart because this may leave bruise marks. Pull the lettuce out of the ground, remove the outer leaves and cut off the worst of the root for the compost bin.

Common mistakes
Failure to thin sufficiently: if you do not, all will end up with small heads or outer leaves only.

ROTATION GROUP A OR C

Space between plants	12–14 in/30–35 cm for Butterheads and Crispheads 8–10 in/20–25 cm for Cos
Space between rows	18–24 in/46–60 cm for Butterheads and Crispheads 12–18 in/30–46 cm for Cos

MARROWS AND SQUASHES
Soil
The best place for marrows is on the compost heap, providing it's in full sun—they need the moisture. The site must be well drained though. Or they are grown in hills prepared the

previous autumn almost entirely of compost with a low nitrogen fertilizer well mixed in.

Sowing

Indoors sow two seeds in each peat pot in April or May. Press the seeds into the growing mix with the pointed end upwards and only just cover. Plant out into hills in June under cloches. Thin to leave the stronger of the two.

Marrows are most successfully grown on the compost heap

Growing
Give them plenty of water all through the growing season. They're deep-rooting plants so give them a really good soaking, applied slowly so that it can reach right down to the roots. Female flowers must be pollinated to produce fruits—pick a male flower and simply push its centre into that of the female flower. The female flowers are easily recognizable by the immature marrows behind them.

Harvesting
Pick marrows when they are still quite small. Test by pushing the thumbnail into one rib of the marrow just above the stalk. If the nail slips in easily the marrow is perfect. Keep on harvesting—the more you pick the more will grow.

Common mistakes
Failure to pollinate. Planting too close. Giving up if the first fruits abort.

ROTATION GROUP A
Space between plants 6–24 in/15–60 cm
Space between rows 36–60 in/1–1·5 m

ONIONS

Onions have more culinary uses than any other vegetable—you can eat them raw or cooked, in salads, stews, soups or pickles, fry them, boil them or even roast them.

Soil
Onions need a deep, friable, well-worked soil, yet you can grow them in the same spot over and over, so once you've done the hard work you can reap your reward for years to come. Dig a trench 10 in/25 cm deep and add in all the compost and well-rotted manure you can, along with some fertilizer. Prepare the ground by mixing these thoroughly into the soil. Allow to settle over winter before planting. In successive years add the same balanced fertilizer and fork in some compost or old manure.

Sowing
There are two ways to grow onions—from seeds or sets.

Sets are simply small onions that have been half-grown the year before and stored. Sow seeds in March or April ½ in/ 1·3 cm deep at 10–15 seeds per ft/30 cm row. If you're using sets, put them in the beds about a week or so later. For extra-large onions sow seed thinly in a heated greenhouse in January or February in boxes or trays, and harden off to plant out in April.

Growing

Onions grow their tops in cool weather and fatten their bulbs in warm weather, so what you want the onions to do is make top-growth during the cool months and start bulbing once the weather warms up in spring. Keep them well watered through their growing season then withhold water. The growing season has stopped when the tops start turning yellow and fall over.

Harvesting

Once the tops start turning yellow you need to go down the rows bending the top-growth over just above the bulb and leave it lying flat on the ground. Bend the tops away from the sun so that the bulbs get as much sunlight as possible. When these tops have shrivelled and gone yellow, lift the bulbs carefully with a fork. Leave them lying on the ground (or on a paved area in wet weather) for a few days to dry out. Then trim off any straggly roots and trim the tops back. Store in a dry place in trays or a wide-mesh bag or hang in a decorative string.

Common mistakes

Planting at the wrong season. Planting in insufficiently prepared ground. Leaving the plants in too long so that growth starts again.

ROTATION GROUP A

Space between plants 2–3 in/5–7·5 cm

Space between rows 12–24 in/30–60 cm

PEAS

If you are going to grow peas, you need to grow them well and spend rather more time on them than on most crops. So if

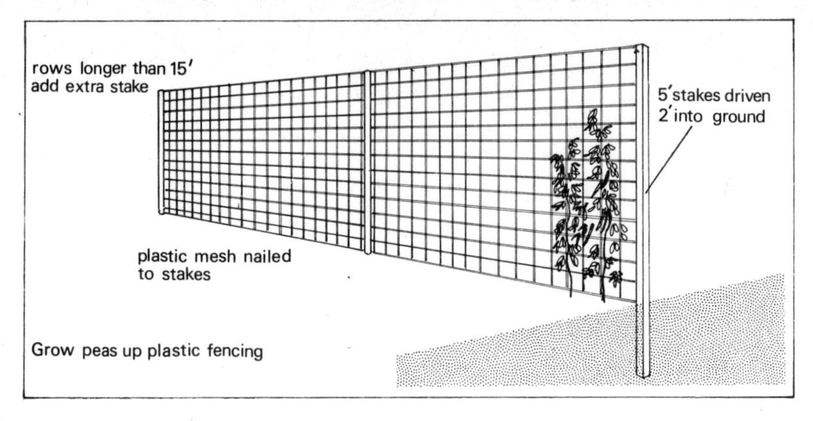

Peas must be supported and the pods held off the ground

you don't like peas all that much, skip them. English peas are a cool season crop, ideal for the UK.

Soil

Peas need an alkaline soil. If you suspect your soil may be on the acid side, test it and apply hydrated lime if necessary. They also need plenty of humus, but very little nitrogen. The best place to plant them is in ground manured for a previous crop, never freshly manured. They like plenty of moisture at the roots, yet like the soil to be well-drained too. (Because of this they are an ideal crop for growing in raised beds, especially since that makes it possible to mix the soil exactly.)

Sowing

Sow seed 2 in/5 cm deep in April till June. Peas usually do best sown where they are to grow. Or if you want an early crop, sow them in peat pots, frames or indoors and plant them out after danger of frost is well gone. Shelter them from chilling winds for a few weeks by putting a hessian or burlap screen on the side of the prevailing wind.

Growing

Two weeks after planting, apply a mulch of compost or peat about 3–4 in/7·5–10 cm deep along the rows. Don't use peat on acid soils—it will make them more acid. For taller-growing

ʼ French beans are ideal for smaller gardens and do not need
g. They produce very heavy crops of excellent flavour

need a good, rich stone-free soil and plenty of moisture
;hout the growing season if large, succulent 'sticks' are to be
ced

One of the modern yellow tomatoes 'Golden Dawn'. The fruits look unripe, but they are exceptionally tasty

'Tiny Tom', perfect for the small garden or for growing in porches or on windowsills

varieties you will need to provide support—traditional pea-sticks are rather untidy, so make a trellis. Drive stout stakes 5 ft/1·6 m tall into the ground at each end of the row, making sure at least 2 ft/60 cm of the pole goes into the ground. On rows more than 15 ft/5 m long put an extra pole in the middle. Nail plastic mesh to the poles. You'll find cultivation easier if you just plant a single row on either side. Keep the soil moist but not soggy. The mulch should help you to keep the weeds down.

Harvesting

Peas are ready when the pods are well-filled and firm. They become hard and lose their sweetness if allowed to harden on the plants. Pick too soon rather than too late. Cut the pods from the haulms: never pull them. Peas are firmly attached to their stalks: if you try to pull them you'll pull the whole plant out. Pick the peas low down on the plant first, those higher up later. When they have finished cropping, put the haulms and roots into the compost because they contain a lot of nitrogen.

Common mistakes

Planting too early: peas can be severely cut back by chilly winds.

ROTATION GROUP A

Space between plants 2–3 in/5–7·5 cm

Space between rows 18–24 in/46–60 cm

PEPPERS

There are two different species of pepper, and you need to know which is which not only because they have different uses in the kitchen but also because one needs higher temperatures than the other. There are sweet peppers (red or green) and there are chillis, capsicums or hot peppers, the fruits of which are much smaller and need hotter summers to grow well.

Soil

Give peppers a sandy, well-drained soil in the sunniest position you can find.

Sowing

Sow indoors only, in April. Sow it shallowly in a soilless growing mix and keep at a temperature not less than 65 °F/ 18 °C. Plant out in June. Don't hesitate to put a cloche over seedlings if you think the weather is likely to become cooler.

Growing

Do not disturb the soil around the plants. Keep weeds down with a mulch of compost, old manure, pine needles, shredded bark or whatever is available. Keep the plants moist at the roots not soggy. As soon as the first flowers appear give the plants some fertilizer, well worked into the mulch. Keep on watering or the plants will drop their flowers. Once there are plenty of peppers don't worry any more about dropping flowers.

Harvesting

Harvest both sorts with secateurs. Do it when the peppers change from green to red if they are to be red peppers. The others you don't need to worry too much about as far as ripeness goes—the real waste is harvesting too late when they start to shrivel and shrink.

Common mistakes

Planting out too early.

ROTATION GROUP A

Space between plants 18–24 in/46–60 cm
Space between rows 24–36 in/60–91 cm

POTATOES

Potatoes are found growing throughout the temperate world. In cash terms they are the most valuable vegetable there is, a part of almost every meal. On top of this, potato growing is good for the soil—it cleans up 'dirty' soil infested with perennial weeds and helps bring it to a good texture for subsequent crops.

Soil

Potatoes will grow in almost any soil but for best results plant them in an acid soil. If the soil has been heavily limed the crop

Seed potatoes should have sturdy prominent eyes.

Side shoots should be rubbed out

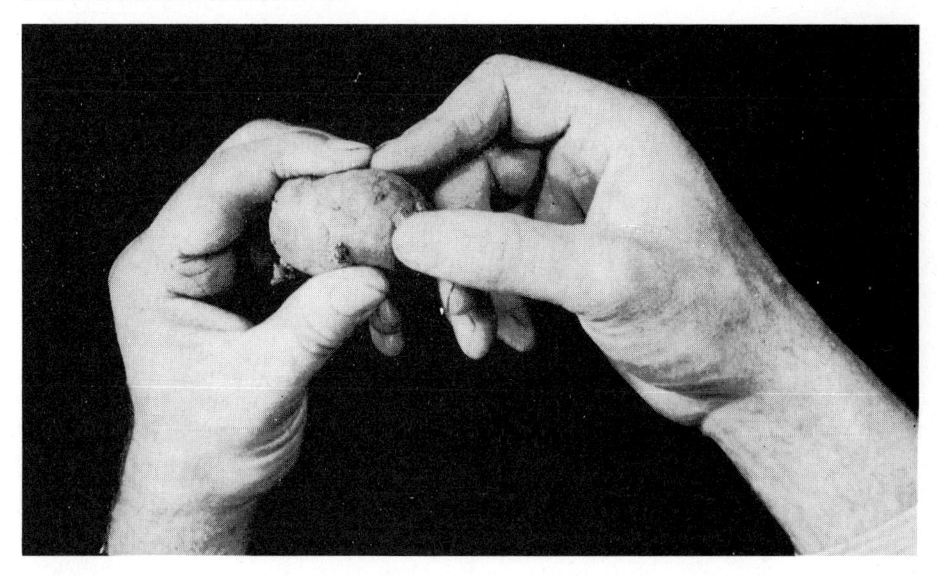

will be small and liable to attack by powdery scab. They prefer light sandy soils, so if yours is on the heavy side, dig in plenty of coarse sand. There's no need to dig manure in, though some humus is a good idea for keeping moisture levels even.

Sowing
You normally buy seed potatoes, dormant tubers. The simplest way is to plant these March–April, about 5 in/12·5 cm deep where they are to grow. If you want to multiply your crop, just cut the tubers into pieces each with one eye, and plant the pieces to get double quantities. If you want an extra early crop, start the tubers indoors before planting out, when the shoots are 4 in/10 cm long.

Growing
The seed potato will grow in two directions at once—sending shoots down and upwards. By harvest time, the original potato will generally have withered. Cultivation is aimed at encouraging the potato to produce long shoots above the tuber, since the longer the shoots the more new potatoes you'll get. It helps a lot to earth up the rows—by building hills in straight rows up to 12 in/30 cm high at planting time. Soil should be heaped up round the shoots so that only the green growing tips show. Earth up every fortnight for six weeks, by which time you should have hills about 12 in/30 cm high along the rows. If you find earthing up a bore pack light, strawy compost or very old manure round the shoots: it'll produce the same results. Orientate the rows north/south to give the crop maximum light.

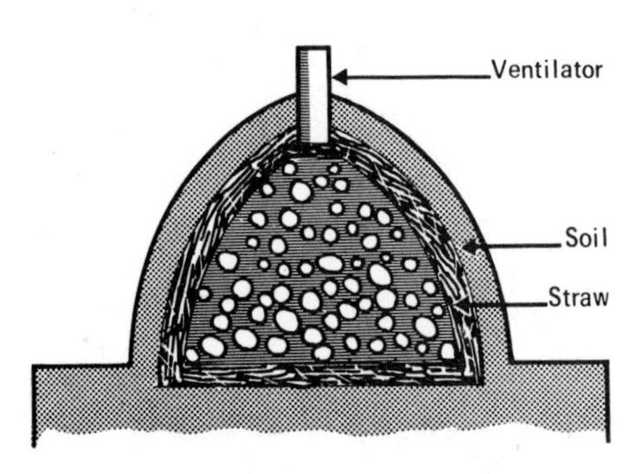

A potato clamp. Note the ventilation shaft; this is essential

Harvesting
The time to harvest potatoes is when the leaves start to turn yellow. Don't wait till they've died off completely. Lift the potatoes by placing a flat pronged fork in the ground a little way from the visible leaves and levering the soil loose. Turn the soil several times and pick out the good fresh potatoes from the soil. After harvesting, level the land and burn the old haulms. Don't compost them: it will start fungal infections.

Common mistakes
Trying to grow potatoes in heavy, wet soils. Letting new tubers be exposed to sunlight, which turns them green, and poisonous.
ROTATION GROUP B
Space between plants 12 in/30 cm
Space between rows 24–36 in/60–92 cm

RADISHES
They're a first-rate crop, no trouble at all. Give a kid a packet of seeds and you'll still get radishes a cordon bleu cook would delight in. It's a popular vegetable right across the world. In some parts it's eaten raw, in others cooked.

Soil
Unlike other rootcrops, radishes like a well-manured soil. This is because they only take three to four weeks from seed to maturity, and any plant that grows that fast needs all the food it can get. Give your radishes a light sandy soil, with lots of compost. At the same time dig in some fertilizer, well and evenly because little patches of it will make the radishes distort.

Sowing
Sow seed in January ½ in/1·3 cm deep in frames, cloches or in the greenhouse. Or sow outdoors from March through to September, making successive sowings, every week or ten days in spring, every two weeks in summer.

Growing
Just keep it moist from seeding to harvest.

Good radishes like these must be grown quickly; otherwise they will turn woody

Harvesting

Pull the radishes from the ground before they reach the size the catalogues say they'll reach. If you wait they will lose some of their crispness. But leave them a little longer and they'll be woody.

Common mistakes

Overplanting. Not harvesting small enough.

ROTATION GROUP B
Space between plants 1–2 in/2·5–5 cm
Space between rows 6–12 in/15–30 cm

SEAKALE BEET, SWISS CHARD

This is the group name for those beets which are grown for their leaves, and used as greens, rather than for their roots. The greens are generally used in much the same way as spinach. In varieties like 'Ruby Chard' the leaves are a rich ruby colour and look particularly bright in the vegetable garden.

Soil

Like crops grown for their roots, it does best in a deeply-worked soil that has been manured for a previous crop. When preparing the soil work in some common salt—in the wild, the plant grows in coastal areas.

Sowing

Sow where the plants are to grow, 1 in/2·5 cm deep in April

Seakale beet can make a tasty alternative to spinach

and then at fortnightly intervals till August. That will give you a succession of crops for about four months.

Growing

Keep the soil weed-free, preferably by applying a low-nutrient value mulch such as garden compost. Keep the moisture level constant: if you try to grow the plants in dry soil the leaves and especially the leaf ribs will be tough and fibrous.

Harvesting

Harvest the outer leaves first, as this allows the inner leaves to grow on to be harvested later. Always pluck the leaves: never cut them. Take the stem between forefinger and thumb as close as possible to the rootstock and detach it with a sharp downward and outward tug.

Common mistakes

Overplanting and underthinning, the usual mistakes with all green crops. Keep notes during the first year to see whether you planted the right amount.

ROTATION GROUP B

Space between plants 4–8 in/10–20 cm

Space between rows 18–24 in/46–60 cm

SPINACH

There are different varieties of spinach and it is important to grow the right one at the right season or you will be faced with the problem of bolting, which is when the spinach sends up its flowerstalk and stops producing the useful leaves.

Soil

Spinach needs a rich, moist soil and a good supply of water at all stages. Since what you want is lots of leaf, grow it in a nitrogen-rich soil, preferably one with plenty of humus in the form of well-rotted manure or compost worked well in.

Sowing

Sow summer spinach in spring, from February to May, making successional sowings every ten days. Sow winter spinach from July to September. Put the seeds in ½ in/1·3 cm deep, for plants to grow 2–4 in/5–10 cm apart and thin out later.

Growing
Keep the weeds down by hoeing: don't mulch. Keep the soil moisture content high for summer spinach, not so high for winter varieties, but in both cases keep this supply even.

Harvesting
The leaves have to be plucked, not pulled. Take the leafstalk between finger and thumb and give it a slight twist at the same time as pulling it downwards and outwards. It should come away cleanly. Keep picking the leaves so long as the plants go on producing succulent ones.

Common mistakes
Sowing the wrong type at the wrong time of year. Sowing too early or too late.
If you want to avoid the problem of bolting, try one of the spinach substitutes:

New Zealand Spinach is a drought-tolerant plant (but still keep the soil moist). Sow from April to July and harvest right through the autumn to winter. The more you pick the more your plant will produce. The leaves and stems can be picked and used just like spinach.

Malabar Spinach is a warm-weather vine, unlike any other spinach in its climbing habit. The leaves are bright green and very glossy and can be harvested and used like spinach all summer. Grow it as a cool greenhouse crop.

Tampala has several different species grown for food. The leaves are sweeter and tastier than ordinary spinach. Sow and cultivate it as for any common garden annual.

ROTATION GROUP A
Space between plants 2–4 in/5–10 cm
Space between rows 12–18 in/30–46 cm

SPROUTS
Brussels sprouts are probably best described as a sort of

Sprouts are greatly improved in flavour by exposure to frost

cabbage which produces dozens of tight little heads in the leaf axils of the stem instead of a large single head of leaves like the normal cabbage. Yield is very high and continues right through the winter, when fresh green vegetables are in short supply.

Soil

You can grow sprouts in literally any fertile soil, in almost pure sand, almost pure gravel or in heavy clay. But of course in poor soils you'll get a poor crop—long leggy plants with loose-leaved sprouts. So prepare the soil as for cabbages, trenching 10 in/25 cm deep and working in plenty of compost or manure and fertilizer. If your soil is on the acid side, add some hydrated lime.

Sowing

Sow thinly in March or April, $\frac{1}{2}$ in/1·3 cm deep, and thin in May/June.

Growing
Sprouts will do fine left to themselves provided you keep them adequately watered and take control measures against cabbage root fly (*see* Cabbage). For best results apply a heavy mulch 3–4 in/7·5–10 cm deep of farmyard manure or compost plus an artificial fertilizer.

Harvesting
Sprouts mature from the bottom of the stem up. To harvest them remove the lowest leaves then gather the sprouts growing at the leaf joints, with a gentle twisting action. Those higher up the stem will mature next.

Common mistakes
Planting too early or too late.
ROTATION GROUP C
Space between plants 12–18 in/30–46 cm
Space between rows 24–30 in/60–75 cm

TOMATOES
You'll probably find tomatoes the most exciting and rewarding of all the vegetables in your garden. But to grow them successfully make sure you choose a suitable variety.

Soil
One problem is that tomatoes are susceptible to a number of wilts and diseases bred in the soil. Avoid this by growing them in new soil each season. The soil should be rich in fertilizer and kept at a high moisture level.

Sowing
If you start tomatoes from seed, the most important thing is to start them early enough. Sow indoors April to May, as shallowly as possible, barely covering the seeds. Sow in peat pots in a soilless growing mix and keep a temperature of at least 60°F/15·6°C, with a fairly high humidity. Plant out in June.

Or you may prefer to buy transplants rather than raise the tomatoes from seed. Make sure you buy them as early as possible, and look for those with stems about the thickness of

An ideal site for outdoor tomato cultivation

a pencil, bushy and compact plants rather than long and drawn out. Avoid any showing yellowing leaves. The main thing to watch for is that night temperatures are not below 50°F/10°C. It is better to delay than risk cold nights. Set the transplants deeper than usual, so that the first leaves are only just showing above the soil. This is so that the part of the stem you bury will sprout extra roots and give the plant more growing and fruiting power.

Growing

If you are growing any of the ordinary varieties, you'll need to train your tomatoes. Outdoors, keep the main stem tied to a stake or let the plant scramble over a trellis or lath framework. In the greenhouse, tie a string to a lath fixed across the astragals and take it down to the base of the plant. Then wind it loosely round the stem and keep winding it as the stem keeps growing. When the plant reaches the top of the string, pinch out the growing tip. Both indoors and out, remove all side shoots, keeping the plant to a single stem (except for bush varieties). Keep the plants to five trusses each. Remove any trusses that form after the end of July: they won't ripen so removing them will help ripen the trusses that have formed earlier. Once fruits start to colour, gradually defoliate the plant, carefully cutting the leaves away from the stem leaving as small a snag as you can. This lets more light get to the fruits and helps them ripen. Don't defoliate too early: the plants need their leaves to use the energy from sunlight for building good fruit trusses.

Harvesting

Trusses ripen from the bottom upwards. You can either remove the fruits as they ripen, or wait till the whole truss is ripe. The fruits snap off readily from the stems. If growing outdoors, remove any trusses that have not ripened fully before your first frost. You can store any fully-formed green tomatoes by wrapping them in newspaper and putting them in a cool place. They'll ripen slowly for a couple of months, then you can finish the process when you want by putting them on the windowsill of a sunny room. After harvesting, uproot the plants and burn them—don't put them on the compost because they are possibly infected and that's the surest way of spreading the infection.

Common mistakes

Growing a variety unsuited to your area or method of cultivation. Planting out too soon or too late. Defoliating the plants too early.

ROTATION GROUP A

Space between plants 18–36 in/46–92 cm
Space between rows 36–60 in/1–1·5 m

Pinching out a tomato sideshoot

3 The Herbs

BASIL

Uses

The leaves are strongly and sweetly aromatic, similar to

Sweet Basil

chives. Use it sparingly because of this powerful flavour. It is most popular in France and Italy for salads and soups, and also in India for curries.

Cultivation

There are two forms of this half-hardy annual. The common form grows up to 3 ft/90 cm and the dwarf form only to 6–9 in/15–22 cm tall and across.

Grow the dwarf form in the greenhouse, sowing seed in March—it will take about two weeks to germinate, and you will probably have an 80 per cent success rate. It is best grown in flats filled with soilless growing mix. As seedlings transplant badly, you will do better if you sow directly into the pots you are going to grow them in, and then thin to one plant per pot.

Alternatively, grow in the garden, lift and pot in September to bring into the greenhouse. Cut them hard back at lifting time. You need to start the crop each year.

BAY

Uses

Bay is an important herb for stews, casseroles and goulashes, or use it in a bouquet garni, which consists of parsley, thyme, the top leaves of celery, a bay leaf, and sage, all wrapped up in a leek leaf, to be suspended in stocks, soups and stews. Bay trees can make interesting and attractive plants if they are grown in tubs or large pots in a sunny spot.

Cultivation

Bay prefers a soil containing lime and is slightly tender. It is best to plant it near a house where it will have protection from the wind and frost, and be able to dig its roots into the foundations to absorb lime from the mortar. Any soil can be tried however, with some success.

Put in young plants in the autumn or spring. Take heel cuttings in April, or 3–4 in/7–10 cm half-ripe cuttings in August. Put in a cold frame, in pots, and pot on as required. Plant out next autumn in a nursery bed for two years. Train to bush or pyramid shape. Clip trained plants twice, in July and September.

Sweet Bay

CHIVES

Uses

This is not strictly speaking a herb, but an onion. It is grown for the 'tip' rather than the bulb. The main culinary use is as a flavouring for baked eggs, soups and salads. The 'tips' should be cut, chopped up and sprinkled over the dish. They are essential for potato salad because their mild flavour of onion is just enough but not too strong.

Chives can also be used for edging a rose border—it is said that roses grow better near them.

Cultivation

Sow seeds outdoors in spring, 10 in/25 cm apart in drills, in

A well-staked row of peas. Pea sticks are becoming increasingly hard to obtain, and plastic netting may be used instead

Onions need a long growing season if large, round globes are to be produced. The top-growth has not fallen over: it is bent over to encourage ripening of the globes

Above: Tubs provide an ideal way of growing herbs in town gardens

Below left: A small herb garden in a cartwheel, a traditional way of growing herbs. *Below right:* A diamond made from floor joists provides an area for growing herbs.

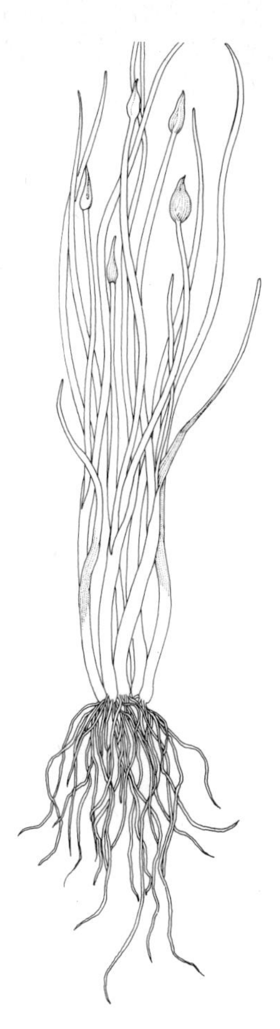
Chives

medium to heavy soil in an open position. Thin to clumps about 6 in/15 cm apart. Transplant in November. Remove the flowers to encourage leaf production. Water well in dry weather and mulch in autumn with garden compost. Cover with cloches if protection is needed from frost.

DILL

Uses

The leaves are used for flavouring salads, fish and vegetables, while the seeds supply gripe water, useful for aiding digestion.

Dill

Cultivation

Sow seed outdoors in March or April in a moist but well-draining soil, in sun. Germination takes fourteen to twenty-one days depending on the soil temperature. Sow also in July for an autumn supply.

Rows should be about 1 ft/30 cm apart. Thin plants to 9 in/22 cm. Dill does not like to be transplanted. Keep well watered to prevent premature flowering.

FENNEL

Uses

The leaves have a strong and unusual flavour, and are used

Fennel

mostly with fish. The basal stems of Florence fennel are also eaten as a vegetable in their own right.

Cultivation

Sow seed outdoors in April in sun or slight shade and a moist, chalky soil. Rows should be $1\frac{1}{2}$–2 ft/45–60 cm and the plants will need staking as they grow. Florence fennel needs a good warm summer, plenty of moisture and a rich soil. The base of the stem should be earthed up as it begins to swell so as to blanch it. For winter use, transplant into pots and keep indoors or under glass.

GARLIC

Garlic

Uses

Like chives, not strictly a herb but an onion. Garlic has the strongest flavour of the onion family and need only be grown in small quantities. It has many good uses, not only for flavouring but in folk cures for colds, catarrh, chest troubles and rheumatism.

In cooking, use it to flavour casseroles or joints, crushing it, not chopping it. Flavour green salads by rubbing a clove of garlic round a wooden bowl, which should not be washed ever, only wiped clean, so as to keep the flavour.

Cultivation

Use new soil each year. Plant four cloves to each 8 in/20 cm pot, in a soilless mix. Keep the pot in a sunny position.

Plant in February or March for an autumn harvest, or September or October for a spring harvest. Keep the plants growing well, but not too moist. Pinch out the flowering shoot. When the leaves turn yellow, tip the pot upside down, pick the new garlic cloves out of the mixture and hang the largest by their leaves, saving the smaller cloves to start the next season's crop.

HORSERADISH

Uses

Horseradish is a plant which has become naturalized in the UK and grows well on commons and road verges—the leaves look like large dock leaves with slightly cut edges.

Horseradish sauce is well known for its use with cold beef, and is made by grating the peppery roots.

Cultivation

Supply a rich, moist soil worked to 2 ft/60 cm deep. Plant 3-in/7-cm root cuttings in March, 1 ft/30 cm apart, and just cover with soil, in a bed separate from other plants: it can be a dangerous weed.

Lift all the plants in late autumn, store the larger roots in sand for cooking, and retain the smaller, also in sand, for planting next spring. Regular plantings ensure the best quality roots for cooking.

Horseradish

MARJORAM, POT

Uses

There are two fairly common marjorams, sweet marjoram which is best grown outdoors and winter or pot marjoram, a semi-shrubby perennial, for winter greenhouse leaves. It can be grown as easily as mint but is not so invasive.

Marjoram is particularly good in rissoles and stuffings. Roasts of poultry and game are improved by rubbing them with crushed leaves of the herb before cooking. Omelettes flavoured with marjoram are excellent but it is not effective in stews, soups or casseroles.

Cultivation

Like other herbs, pot marjoram can be grown from seed, but is probably easier if bought as a plant from a nursery or garden centre.

Root the cuttings in a cold frame or in a propagation case

with a little bottom heat. Pot into 5-in/12-cm pots for the greenhouse. The leaves can be picked all winter. Prune hard back in late summer. You can grow it on to 10-in/25-cm pot size, but you'll get tastier leaves if you start new plants each spring.

MINT

Uses

There are two main kinds of mint important for cooking. Spearmint, which has long narrow dark green leaves, is best for mint sauce with lamb, while apple mint, with furry rounded leaves, is best for flavouring new potatoes, or in drinks.

Cultivation

Plant between autumn and spring. Propagate by division at these seasons as well, or lift rooted stems and plant these.

Mint

Damp soil is best.

Mint grows so easily that it needs curbing rather than encouraging. One good method is to grow it in a box. Or if it is grown in the garden surround it by a barrier—pieces of slate, for example, or a big polythene bag with holes cut in the base for drainage, or strips of corrugated iron.

PARSLEY

Uses

The leaves have a strongly distinctive flavour, widely used in cooking. It contains quite a large amount of vitamin C and is of good nutritional value.

Parsley

Parsley is most commonly used for parsley sauce. It is also an essential ingredient of a bouquet garni (*see* BAY) to flavour soups, stews and stocks.

Cultivation

Parsley has to be sown every year as it is an annual. Sow in the spring for a summer crop, in moist fertile soil and sun or shade. Rows should be 1 ft/30 cm apart, with 6 in/15 cm between plants. A warm soil will speed germination, which can take from 10 to 28 days. A good tip is to run a kettle of boiling water along the drill. For winter use, sow in July, and protect with cloches if frost or snow is expected. Remove the flower-heads to encourage the leaves to grow.

ROSEMARY

Uses

Pork and veal are vastly improved if flavoured with rosemary. Combined with tarragon and lemon rind, it makes an excellent seasoned flour for oven-fried chicken.

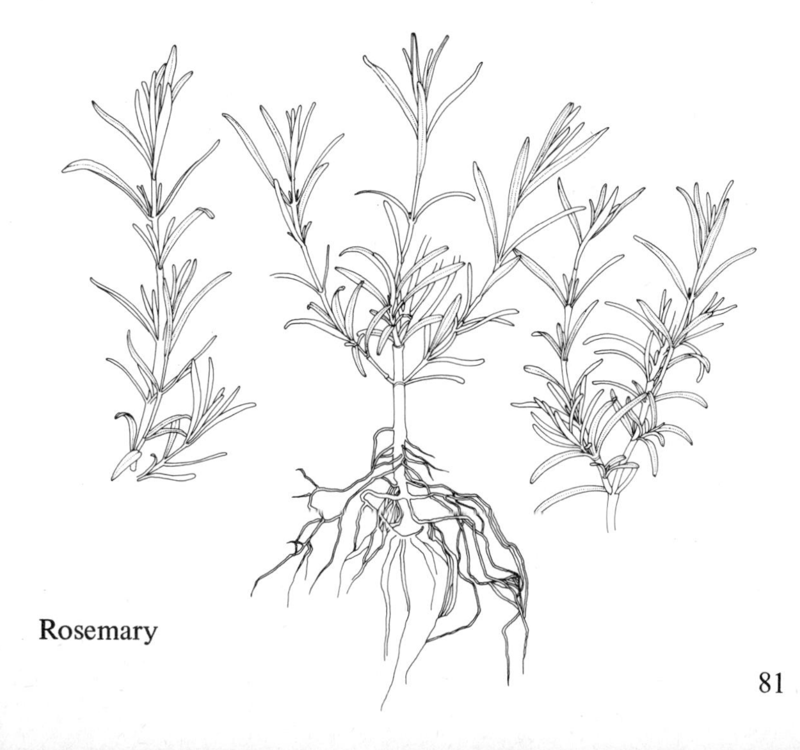

Rosemary

Cultivation

Rosemary is an aromatic evergreen shrub, growing to about 4 ft/1 m high. In the greenhouse either pot on by stages to a 15-in/36-cm pot, keeping it to size by cutting it back hard each spring; or grow it anew in a 5-in/12-cm pot each year.

Propagate by tip cuttings in March. Put four round the edge of a 4-in/10-cm pot in a cold frame or propagating case. Cuttings taken in August can also be successful, but usually take longer to root.

Plants enjoy a shady soil, and do best kept rather on the dry side. Keep drier in winter than in summer.

Though it will survive most winters outdoors in southern districts of the UK it is not reliably hardy.

Broad Leaved Sage

SAGE

Uses

Sage's strongly aromatic, slightly bitter leaves are often used in cooking, particularly with pork or duck, or in kebabs along with the meat, mushrooms and tomatoes. It is best known for its combination with onion as a stuffing.

There is a purple-leaved form which can be as decorative as any house plant, and it is attractive in flower also, but if you want the sage for flavouring, don't allow it to flower.

Cultivation

Plant in the spring, in well-drained soil and a sunny position. Avoid a heavy wet soil.

It can easily be grown from seed sown in late April, which takes about three weeks to germinate. Or increase from 3-in/8-cm cuttings taken in August and put in a cold frame. Pot on singly and plant out the following spring.

SORREL

Uses

The rather bitter leaves are very good for soup, but should

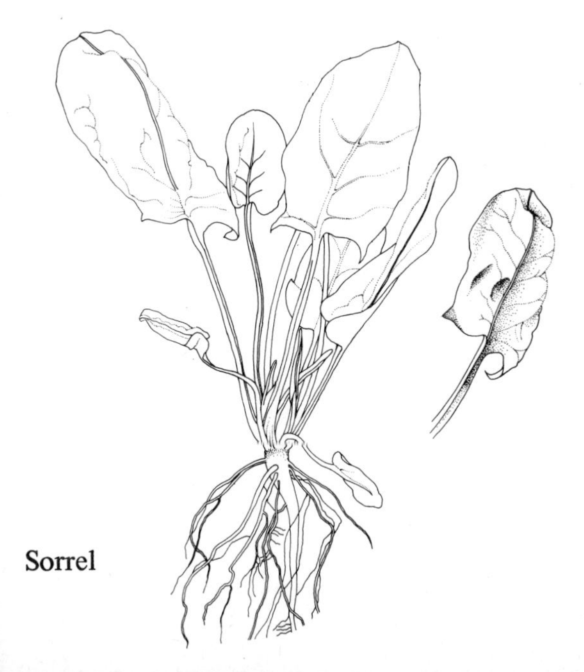

Sorrel

otherwise be used sparingly as they are so strong tasting. It is said to contain a good amount of vitamin C.

Cultivation

Plant in spring or early autumn in moist, slightly heavy soil, allowing 1 ft/30 cm between plants. Remove the flowering stems to encourage leaf production. Divide in spring or sow seed in April, thinning when large enough to handle.

TARRAGON

Uses

Tarragon has a flavour all its own, faintly like aniseed. There are two kinds—the true French tarragon is the only form which has the right flavour, what is known as Russian or English tarragon has no taste at all.

French tarragon has many cooking uses: particularly for chicken in a casserole or oven fried, in a seasoned flour combined with rosemary and lemon rind. It is perhaps best known for tarragon vinegar, for making mayonnaise sauce, and for sauce tartare or continental mustard.

Cultivation

A well-drained, even dryish soil, is essential and preferably a sunny sheltered place.

Plant in spring or September at 2 ft/60 cm apart and transplant about four years after the original planting to maintain the flavour. Increase by division in spring. Seed does not set in this country. Protect in severe weather.

THYME

Uses

The highly aromatic leaves are often used with meat and any savoury dish. Thyme can be combined with parsley to make a stuffing for poultry or it can go into a bouquet garni. It is also a herb used in the liqueur Benedictine.

Cultivation

It is easily grown by division in spring, or from 2-in/5-cm cuttings taken in early summer, put in a frame and potted on when rooted. Plant out in September.

Seed can be sown in spring (not lemon thyme) and treated in the same way, the final distance between plants being 1 ft/30 cm either way. A sunny place and a light soil are preferred, alkaline if possible. It is a good container plant.

Thyme

4 Freezing Vegetables

All vegetables to be frozen should be young and tender, and they are best picked and frozen in small amounts.

Vegetables to be frozen must be blanched to arrest the working of enzymes (types of protein in foods which speed up chemical reactions). Blanching at high heat stops the enzymes from affecting quality, flavour, colour and nutritive value during storage. Unblanched vegetables can be stored for up to three months in the freezer, but the effect of freezing will be the same as that of an early frost, and they will lose their colour and texture. Unblanched vegetables also require the full cooking time, unlike blanched vegetables which are already partly cooked.

PREPARATION FOR FREEZING

All vegetables must first be washed thoroughly in cold water, then cut or sorted into similar sizes. If more are picked than can be dealt with at one time, they should be put into polythene bags in a refrigerator.

BLANCHING

There are two forms of blanching: (a) by water; (b) by steam. Steam blanching is not recommended for leafy green vegetables which tend to mat together, and it takes longer than water blanching, though it conserves more minerals and vitamins. Blanching should be timed carefully, though inaccuracy will not be disastrous. Too little blanching may result in colour change and in a loss of nutritive value; too much blanching will mean a loss of crispness and fresh flavour.

(*a*) *Water blanching*. Blanch only 1lb vegetables at a time to ensure thoroughness and to prevent a quick change in the temperature of the water. Use a saucepan holding at least 8 pints/4 litres of water. Bring the water to the boil while the vegetables are being prepared. Put vegetables into a wire basket, chip pan, salad shaker or a muslin bag and completely immerse in the saucepan of fast-boiling water; cover tightly and keep the heat high under the saucepan until blanching is completed. Check carefully the time needed for each vegetable (see pages 89–94) and time blanching from when water returns to boiling point. As soon as the full blanching time has elapsed, remove vegetables and drain at once. Bring water to boiling point again before dealing with another batch of vegetables.
(*b*) *Steam blanching*. Put enough water into the saucepan below a steamer to prevent any risk of it boiling dry. Prepare the vegetables, and when the water is boiling fast put the wire basket or muslin bag into steamer. Cover tightly, and count steaming time from when the steam escapes from the lid. Steam blanching takes half as long again as water blanching (e.g. 2 minutes water blanching equals 3 minutes steam).

COOLING

Cooling must be done immediately after blanching, and it must be very thorough indeed; before being packed for the freezer, the vegetables should be cool right through to the centre. The time taken is generally equal to the blanching time if a large quantity of cold water is used. It is best to ice-chill this water, and it is a good idea to prepare large quantities of ice the day before a vegetable freezing session is planned. Vegetables which are not cooled quickly become mushy, as they will go on cooking in their own heat. After cooling in the water, the vegetables should be thoroughly drained, and preferably finished off on absorbent paper.

PACKING

Pack the cooled food in usable quantities to suit family or entertaining needs. Vegetables can be packed in bags or boxes; the chosen method will depend on the storage space available, as bagged vegetables are more difficult to keep, though obviously cheaper to prepare.

Vegetables are normally packed dry, though wet-packing in brine is believed to prevent some vegetables toughening in storage, and non-leafy varieties can be packed in this way. The vegetables are packed into rigid containers to within 1 in/ 2·5 cm of the top, and are then just covered with brine, made in the proportion of 2 tablespoons/2 × 15 ml spoons salt per quart/litre of water, leaving ½-in/1·3-cm headspace. It may be found in hard-water areas that home-frozen vegetables are consistently tough, and it is then worth trying brine.

COOKING

The best results are obtained from cooking vegetables immediately on removal from the freezer. When cooking unthawed vegetables, break the block into 4 or 5 pieces when removing from the carton, to allow heat to penetrate evenly and rapidly.

One or two vegetables such as broccoli and spinach are better cooked partially thawed, and corn on the cob needs complete thawing. If vegetables are thawed, they should be cooked at once.

Partial cooking during blanching, and the tenderizing process produced by temperature changes during storage, reduce the final cooking time of frozen vegetables. In general, they should cook in one-third to one-half the time allowed for fresh vegetables. Very little water, if any, should be used for cooking frozen vegetables; about ¼ pint/125 ml to 1 lb/500 g vegetables, depending on variety, is plenty. The water should be boiling, the vegetables covered at once with a lid, and as soon as boiling point is reached again, the vegetables should be simmered gently for the required time. Since flavour is always lost into the cooking water, some cooks prefer to steam vegetables, cook them in a double boiler, or to bake or fry them. For baking, the vegetables should be separated and drained, then put into a greased casserole with a knob of butter and seasoning, covered tightly and baked at 350 °F/ 180 °C Gas Mark 4 for about 30 minutes. For frying, the vegetables remain frozen, and are put into a heavy frying pan containing 1 oz/25 g melted butter. The pan must be tightly covered and the vegetables cooked gently until they separate, then cooked over moderate heat until cooked through and tender, being turned as required to prevent burning.

Here are notes on preparing, packing, storing and cooking various kinds of vegetables. The blanching times given are for water blanching:

Beans (French)

Preparation and packing. Remove tops and tails, leaving small beans whole, and cutting bigger ones into 1 in/2·5 cm pieces. Blanch whole beans 3 minutes, cut beans 2 minutes. Cool and pack in polythene bags.
Thawing and serving. Cook whole beans for 7 minutes in boiling salted water; cook cut beans for 5 minutes.
Storage time. 12 months.

Beans (Runner)

Preparation and packing. Cut beans in pieces and blanch 2 minutes, cool and pack in polythene bags.
Thawing and serving. Cook 7 minutes in boiling salted water.
Storage time. 12 months.
Special notes. If runner beans are shredded finely before freezing, the cooked result will be pulpy and tasteless.

Beetroot

Preparation and packing. Only very young beetroot under 3 in/7·5 cm in diameter are suitable for freezing. Cook in boiling water until tender, putting larger beetroot in water first and adding the remainder in graduated sizes at 10-minute intervals. Cool quickly in running water, rub off skins and pack in cartons. Beetroot under 1 in/2·5 cm diameter may be frozen whole; large ones should be sliced or diced.
Thawing and serving. Thaw in cartons in refrigerator for 2 hours, drain and add dressing.
Storage time. 6–8 months.
Special notes. Short blanching and long storage make beetroot rubbery, so complete cooking is essential.

Broccoli

Preparation and packing. Compact heads with tender stalks not more than 1 in/2·5 cm thick should be used, and these heads should be uniformly green. Trim woody stems and take off outer leaves. Wash well and soak in salt water (2 teaspoons/

2 × 5 ml spoons salt to 8 pints/4 litres water) to clear out insects, for 30 minutes. Wash in fresh water. Cut into sprigs and blanch 3 minutes for thin stems, 4 minutes for medium stems, 5 minutes for thick stems. Pack into bags or boxes, with half the heads at each end.
Thawing and serving. Plunge frozen heads into boiling water and cook for 8 minutes.
Storage time. 12 months.

Brussels Sprouts
Preparation and packing. Use small compact heads and grade well before blanching. Clean and wash well. Blanch 3 minutes for small sprouts, 4 minutes for medium sprouts; cool and pack in cartons or bags.
Thawing and serving. Cook frozen sprouts for 8 minutes in boiling water.
Storage time. 12 months.

Cabbage (Green and Red)
Preparation and packing. Use young crisp cabbage. Wash thoroughly and shred finely. Blanch $1\frac{1}{2}$ minutes, and pack in polythene bags.
Thawing and serving. Cook for 8 minutes in boiling salted water.
Storage time. 6 months.
Special notes. Frozen cabbage should not be used raw for salads.

Carrots
Preparation and packing. Use very young carrots, wash thoroughly and scrape. They may be packed whole, sliced or diced. Blanch whole small carrots (or cut carrots) for 3 minutes. Pack in cartons or polythene bags, leaving $\frac{1}{2}$-in/1·3-cm headspace in cartons.
Thawing and serving. Cook frozen carrots for 8 minutes in boiling water.
Storage time. 12 months.

Cauliflower
Preparation and packing. Heads should be firm and compact

with close white flowers. Wash and break into small sprigs. Add the juice of a lemon to blanching to keep cauliflower white. Blanch 3 minutes, cool, and pack in lined boxes or polythene bags.
Thawing and serving. Cook for 10 minutes in boiling water.
Storage time. 6 months.

Celery
Preparation and packing. Use crisp young stalks, removing any strings. Scrub well and remove dirt under running water. Cut in 1-in/2·5-cm lengths and blanch for 3 minutes. Drain, cool, and pack in polythene bags. Celery may also be packed in rigid containers covered with flavoured water used for blanching, leaving ½-in/1·3-cm headspace.
Thawing and serving. Add to stews or soups, or cook as a vegetable, using its own liquid if frozen by this method.
Storage time. 6 months.
Special notes. Since celery must be blanched for freezing, it cannot then be used for raw salads and snacks, but it is useful for cooked dishes.

Corn on the Cob
Preparation and packing. Corn must be fresh and tender. It may be frozen as cobs or kernels.
Cobs should be graded when leaves and siik threads are removed, and stems cut short. They should not be starchy or over-ripe, nor have shrunken or under-sized kernels. Blanch 4 minutes for small cobs, 6 minutes for medium cobs, and 8 minutes for large cobs. Cool and dry, and pack individually in freezer paper or foil. Freeze immediately in coldest part of freezer, then pack in bags.
Kernels can be scraped from blanched cobs and packed in cartons leaving ½-in/1·3-cm headspace.
Thawing and serving. Correct cooking after freezing is particularly important with corn.

1 Put frozen corn in enough cold water to cover it completely. Put on high heat, bring to a fast boil and simmer for 5 minutes.
2 Thaw in wrappings in refrigerator, plunge in boiling water and cook for 10 minutes.

3 Preheat oven to 350 °F/180 °C Gas Mark 4 and roast for 20 minutes, or wrap in foil to roast on a barbecue, turning frequently.

Storage time. 12 months.

Kale

Preparation and packing. Use young, tender, tightly curled kale, discarding dry or tough leaves. Remove leaves from stems and blanch 1 minute. Cool, drain, and chop if liked. Pack tightly into containers or bags leaving ½-in/1·3 cm head-space.

Thawing and serving. Cook frozen kale in boiling water for 8 minutes.

Storage time. 6 months.

Kohlrabi

Preparation and packing. Use mild-flavoured kohlrabi which is not too large but is young and tender. Trim, wash and peel, leaving small ones whole, and dicing large ones. Blanch whole vegetables for 3 minutes; diced for 2 minutes. Cool and pack in polythene bags or containers, leaving ½-in/1·3-cm head-space for diced vegetables.

Thawing and serving. Cook frozen kohlrabi for 10 minutes in boiling water.

Storage time. 12 months.

Peas

Preparation and packing. Use young sweet peas which are not old or starchy. Shell, and blanch 1 minute, lifting blanching basket in and out of water to distribute heat evenly through the layers of peas. Chill quickly and pack in polythene bags or rigid containers.

Edible-pod peas should be flat and tender. Wash well, and remove both ends and any strings. Blanch ½ minute in small quantities so peas remain crisp.

Thawing and serving. Cook frozen shelled peas or frozen edible pods for 7 minutes in boiling water.

Storage time. 12 months.

Peppers (Green and Red)

Preparation and packing. Freeze green and red peppers separ-

ately or in mixed packages. They may be frozen in halves for stuffing, or in slices for use in stews or sauces. Wash well, cut off stems and caps, remove seeds and membranes. Blanch halves 3 minutes, slices 2 minutes. Pack in rigid containers or polythene bags.
Roast red peppers may be prepared by grilling under a high heat until skin is charred, then plunging into cold water and rubbing off skins. Remove caps and seeds, and pack tightly in rigid containers in salt solution (1 tablespoon/1 × 15 ml spoon salt to 1 pint/500 ml water) leaving 1-in/2·5-cm headspace.
Canned peppers which are left unused may be frozen in small containers in liquid from the can.
Thawing and serving. Thaw uncooked peppers for 1½ hours at room temperature before using. Roasted peppers should be thawed in their containers, in the salt solution, then drained and dressed with olive oil and seasoning.
Storage time. 12 months.

Potatoes
Preparation and packing. Potatoes are best frozen when small and new, or in cooked form as chips, croquettes, baked potatoes or Duchesse potatoes.
New potatoes should be scraped and washed, blanched 4 minutes, cooled and packed in polythene bags. They may also be slightly undercooked, drained, tossed in butter, cooled quickly and packed.
Mashed potatoes can be made with butter and hot milk, and frozen in bags or waxed cartons. The same mixture can be used for *Croquettes* to be fried, drained and cooled before packing.
Chips should be cooked in clean odour-free fat, drained on paper, cooled and packed in polythene bags.
Thawing and serving. Cook *new potatoes* in boiling water for 15 minutes; *buttered new potatoes* can be reheated by plunging the freezing bag in boiling water, removing from heat and leaving for about 10 minutes.
Mashed potatoes should be reheated in a double boiler, or can be slightly thawed, then spread on meat or fish cooked in the oven. *Croquettes* should be thawed for two hours at room

temperature before heating at 350 °F/180 °C Gas Mark 4 for 20 minutes.
Chips may be heated in a frying pan with a little hot fat, or on a baking tray at 300 °F/150 °C Gas Mark 2 for 12 minutes.
Storage time. New potatoes 12 months; cooked potatoes 3 months.

Spinach
Preparation and packing. Use young tender spinach, remove stems and discoloured or bruised leaves. Wash very well and blanch 2 minutes, shaking blanching basket so that leaves separate. Cool quickly and press out excess moisture. Pack in rigid containers, leaving ½-in/1·3-cm headspace, or in polythene bags.
Thawing and serving. Melt a little butter in a heavy pan, and cook frozen spinach for 7 minutes.
Storage time. 12 months.

Tomatoes
Preparation and packing. Tomatoes should not be frozen for salad use, but are good for cooking. They are most usefully frozen in the form of pulp, but can also be frozen whole or as juice.
Whole tomatoes should be wiped clean, the stems removed, and the tomatoes packed in usable quantities in polythene bags.
Tomato pulp is best prepared by skinning and coring tomatoes, then simmering them in their own juice for 5 minutes until soft. Sieve, cool and pack in small containers.
Tomato juice is made from cored and quartered ripe tomatoes simmered with a lid on for 10 minutes. Put through muslin, cool and pack into cartons leaving 1-in/2·5-cm headspace.
Thawing and serving. Thaw *whole tomatoes* at room temperature for 2 hours before cooking. Thaw *purée* in container at room temperature for 2 hours before using, or turn frozen purée into soup or stew as required in the recipe being followed. Thaw *juice* in its container in the refrigerator and serve a little frosty, seasoned to taste.
Storage time. Whole tomatoes 10–12 months; purée 12 months; juice 12 months.

5 Harvesting, Preserving, Storing and Cooking Herbs

With a supply of herbs in your garden and the knowledge of how to harvest, preserve and store them, you can make sure of having the flavours you require for cooking throughout the year. What's more, you will be able to turn to your winter store for beauty aids and soothing drinks when fresh herbs are unobtainable. Preserving herbs is not difficult. There was a time when every housewife would know about such things. Drying is the most commonly used method and is very good, and those who own a home-freezer will find that many basic herbs can be 'put on ice' so to speak until they are needed.

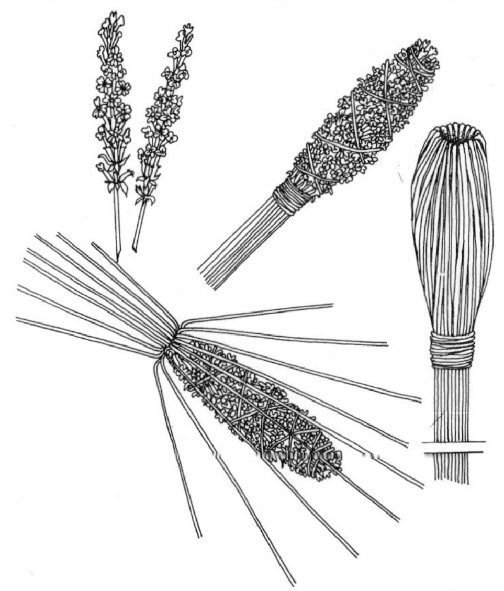

Harvesting might sound a rather grandiose word if you have but a few herbs in pots on your window ledge, but it applies just as much to gathering in a few stems as it does to vast quantities. In any case, you must never pick or cut more herbs to be dried—or frozen—at any one time than can easily be dealt with.

Where the leaves are to be preserved cut just before the herb comes into flower. The reason for this is that much of the strength of the plant would go into the flowers and you wouldn't get such a tasty end-product. Left until after the flowers have faded you get the problem of what to do with the stems and seeds. If the worst comes to the worst and you return from a holiday to find the season more advanced than you expected and the herbs already in flower, you can still manage, even mixing flowers and leaves in together. This will not give a first-class result, either for colour or flavour, but would 'do'.

Herbs should not be cut on a wet day; choose a bright sunny one. Leave it until after the dew has disappeared so the foliage is dry, and pick before the sun gets very hot.

Using a sharp implement, where necessary, you can cut the stems of small-leaved plants to make life easier for drying and dealing with the herb later on. Large leaves can be picked individually but whatever you do, be careful not to damage them, especially the fragrant ones which suffer from bruising.

DRYING

Marjoram and thyme are easy herbs to dry. When picking basil always keep some leaves on the plant as this seems to

encourage others to grow. Be careful leaves do not darken. If drying in bunches, 2–3 sprigs per bunch, no more. Chives are far better used fresh or frozen. Dill and fennel leaves can be dried but are best for their seeds. Parsley requires care, and should be picked before it bolts.

Plants from which the seeds are to be harvested should be left until the heads turn brown. You have to watch your timing carefully or the seeds will fall and scatter. Better be early than late. Pick on a dry day. Dill, and fennel, are good for their seeds.

Garlic is something of an exception as far as drying herbs is concerned. Harvest in the autumn. Leave it on top of the ground or in a warm, (not hot) dry atmosphere until ready, then store in a cool, airy place as you do onions.

Herbs that are to be home-frozen should be picked when young and very fresh, and dealt with as quickly as possible.

Drying really means that the herbs need to be in a steady warm temperature with the dry air circulating all the time to take away moisture, and there should be no risk of condensation. Drying in the sun, which might sound tempting, is not always effective and can mar the colour. Generally, the more quickly herbs are dried the more of their aroma is preserved.

Most homes have plenty of suitable spots. An attic which is warmed by the sun, that is clean and airy and which doesn't suffer from quick heat loss at night; a spare room; an airing cupboard; the cooker; the kitchen; a garage which is not likely

to be filled with petrol fumes, can all be used successfully; always avoid placing herbs in the sun's rays.

You can tie herbs, keeping each variety to itself, in bunches and hang them up to dry. Keep bundles small. They could become mildewed in the middle if too full. When there is a danger of them becoming dusty, cover them with fine muslin. You know the herbs are clean to start with; if not you will have to wash them first, then leave them to dry again.

Bunches take between 14–21 days to get crisp and brittle, at which stage they are ready to be prepared for storing.

Seeds have to be looked after, too. Cut the tops off the plants with the seed heads attached and lay them carefully on prepared trays, then cover with clean, dry pieces of linen or cotton and leave in a warm, airy room until the seeds loosen. Beat out the seeds with a stick and lay them to dry in an evenly warm spot where the temperature must not go above 70 °F. Turn them over daily. When fully dry they can be stored.

CONTAINERS

Before you get around to storing herbs you must make sure you have an adequate supply of containers. Small glass jars with tight-fitting lids or corks are ideal, and these must be spotlessly clean and dry.

If you intend to keep herbs on the sprig, (sage, thyme, rosemary are excellent for this and useful for making bunches of herbs, or for putting into vinegars or oils as decoration) you do need suitably-sized jars.

COOKING WITH HERBS

Certain herbs have become associated with different foods. Be guided, but not dominated, by this association. Start with small quantities, as over-flavouring is unsatisfactory. A herb should complement and blend into a recipe, not be an over-powering element in it; and the amount that suits one person might not please another. So using 'a pinch', that is a quarter of a level teaspoonful, makes sense as a beginning.

You will also have to adjust the quantities according to whether you are using freshly picked, dried or frozen herbs, and realize that some are far stronger than others.

Generally speaking, dried have a more concentrated flavour than fresh herbs, so use less; frozen ones don't have quite such a pronounced taste as those taken straight from the garden, so you might have to use more.

Parsley, mint, lemon thyme can be used without too much thought; chives too, if you like a slightly oniony touch.

Tarragon, thyme, bay leaves and marjoram have strong flavours and should be used sparingly.

Now let us have a look at which herbs to use with what.

Beef:	Horseradish, basil, marjoram, thyme, rosemary.
Pork and Bacon:	Sage, basil, rosemary, chives, parsley, bay.
Lamb:	Rosemary, garlic, dill, bay.
Veal:	Thyme, sage, rosemary.
Stews:	Bay, dill, garlic, horseradish, marjoram, parsley, thyme, sage, rosemary, tarragon, chives.
Soups:	Basil (especially for tomato or turtle) mint (especially for pea), parsley, thyme, bay, fennel (for fish).
Poultry:	Parsley, sage, tarragon, thyme, rosemary, fennel.
Fish:	Fennel, sage, parsley, basil, chives.
Eggs:	Chives, tarragon, marjoram, basil, parsley.
Hard Cheeses:	Basil, thyme, sage.
Soft Cheeses:	Mint, dill, sage, basil, chives, garlic, parsley.
Salads:	Chives, fennel, tarragon, thyme, garlic, sage, dill foliage.
Pasta:	Basil, garlic, mint, parsley, thyme.
Cabbage:	Parsley.
Peas:	Mint.
Carrots:	Mint, basil, parsley.
Potatoes:	Mint, parsley, chives, garlic.
Spinach:	Mint.
Beans:	Sage, parsley.
Tomatoes:	Basil, marjoram, chives, parsley.
Stuffings:	Parsley, sage, thyme (lemon thyme good with veal).

Sauces:	Bay, dill (for fish), fennel (for fish), garlic, mint, parsley, horseradish.
Teas and Vinegars:	As you wish (tarragon famous for vinegar).
Breads, Cakes, Biscuits:	Rosemary, basil
Desserts:	Mint, bay, dill.
Jams and Jellies:	Mint, parsley
Cold Drinks and Cups:	Mint, rosemary.
Garnishes:	Parsley, mint, thyme, rosemary, basil, chives.

Index